Handbook of
American Aging
Programs

Handbook
of
American
Aging
Programs

edited by

Lorin A. Baumhover

and

Joan Dechow Jones

foreword by

Congressman Walter Flowers

GREENWOOD PRESS
Westport, Connecticut • London, England

Library of Congress Cataloging in Publication Data

Main entry under title:

Handbook of American aging programs.

Includes index.
1. Gerontology—Addresses, essays, lectures. 2. Aged—Legal status, laws, etc.—United States—Addresses, essays, lectures. 3. Aged— Medical care—United States—Addresses, essays, lectures. 4. Social work with the aged—United States—Addresses, essays, lectures. 5. Evaluation research (Social action programs)—United States— Addresses, essays, lectures. I. Baumhover, Lorin A. II. Jones, Joan Dechow.

HQ1064.U5h22   362.6   76-28641
ISBN 0-8371-9287-0

Library of Congress Catalog Card Number: 76-28641
ISBN: 0-8371-9287-0

First published in 1977

Greenwood Press, Inc.
51 Riverside Avenue, Westport, Connecticut 06880

Printed in the United States of America

CONTENTS

Part IV: ADVOCACY AND OMBUDSMAN PROGRAMS

FOREWORD

The elderly—those persons aged sixty-five and over—comprise America's fastest growing minority group, a minority group that we all hope to join eventually. In 1900, persons sixty-five and older constituted only 4 percent of our population. Now the figure is more than 10 percent, and it probably will reach 15 percent by the year 2000. The average American in 1900 could expect to live only forty-nine years, but now the life expectancy is seventy-one years and is increasing.

For decades, many older Americans suffered from lack of attention to problems endemic to the aged. Successive advances in medical science prolonged lives, but there was little research into the aging process, the diseases of old age, and the special physical and emotional problems and needs of older persons. Except for Social Security, the federal government almost totally failed to recognize that a problem existed.

Happily, during the 1960s, government at all levels and Americans as a whole became more sensitive and responsive to the needs of the elderly.

In 1965, the Congress set up the Medicare program, under which millions of Americans receive federal assistance in meeting hospital and doctor bills, and the Older Americans Act, which established the Administration on Aging and authorized a variety of programs to help elderly Americans.

In the years that followed, more legislation was passed. During this period, the Retired Senior Volunteer Program was established, as were programs to provide elderly Americans with hot, nutritious meals and part-time jobs, and to keep them at home and out of hospitals and nursing homes. The Congress also passed the Pension Reform Act and the Age Discrimination Act, set up the National Institute on Aging, and created the House Select Committee on Aging as a counterpart to the Senate's Special Committee on Aging established earlier.

At the same time, state and local governments set up agencies and organizations to operate programs to help the elderly, and thousands of volunteers at the neighborhood and community levels began offering assistance.

With the advent of hundreds of programs that spend billions of dollars to help millions of people, there has arisen a growing need for a text or handbook to serve as a guide in this area. This excellent work, edited by my good friends Joan Jones and Lorin Baumhover, will provide a much needed perspective on how these programs fit together. It will be of tremendous value both to those involved in the study of aging and to those providing services for the elderly.

All Americans—not just our public officials, not just our authorities on aging, but all of us—need to work toward a long-range policy to insure the economic, physical, and emotional well-being of the elderly. We must not let them down. After all, it was their hard work, imagination, perseverance, and sacrifice that helped our nation become what it is today. Our older Americans are people of experience, hope, and wisdom, and we desperately need their talent and energy in this difficult period of American history.

Congressman Walter Flowers
Member of the House Select
Committee on Aging

INTRODUCTION

Since the passage of the Older Americans Act of 1965, an increasingly large and complex number of programs for older adults has been begun at state and local levels. To the direct service provider or program administrator new to the field of aging, this wide range of programs is frequently an indecipherable puzzle. Often the only sources of program information are government publications written in unfamiliar and difficult technical language.

In assessing the need for a guide to aging programs to bridge the gap between the highly technical and the everyday, practical resource tools for those just introduced to the field of aging, we decided on a handbook format. The decisions on which programs the handbook should include were based on our collective experience in conducting in-service training programs for professionals in aging and in planning for the implementation of state and community aging programs.

Questions that we were most frequently asked also helped establish a frame of reference for the book. These were basic information-seeking and how-to questions that focused on the need of translating federal rules and regulations into programs for people. Therefore, this handbook does not present an exhaustive discussion of American aging programs but relates to the need for basic information. Aside from mere facts, both practitioners and students need to know how programs on aging are implemented in the community. We decided to address ourselves to these two needs for clear program descriptions and how-to information; accordingly, we requested articles from professionals experienced in the field of aging. These professionals are from both academic and program areas and represent various social service agencies. The contributions included here provide an analysis of selected programs, and to avoid parochialism, they came from professionals in various parts of the country. The objective of this book, then, is not to provide a definitive or critical examination of American aging programs, but to look closely at a number of programs that are having a significant impact on the lives of older adults in America today.

In one sense, aging in contemporary America may be defined by the programs designed for the elderly. The functional definition of satisfactory aging might be stated as the involvement of older people in organized efforts designed specifically for them. In other words, "good" aging may be involvement in an ACTION program or as a senior aide or as a participant in a retired person's association. It may also be attending a Title VII nutrition program or serving as a volunteer board member. In other words, a functional definition of satisfactory aging may not require the usual measures utilized in the social sciences.

The field of gerontology is new, and perhaps identifying it as a science is not accurate. There are considerable gaps in gerontological research and certainly so in the development of a theoretical base. To fill these gaps is not the goal of this book. Rather, the goal is to review ongoing programs on aging that are also new. Most workers in gerontology maintain that old age is not necessarily a problem, that perhaps it is a condition or a variable, or even a time in life characterized by incidents that do not characterize other times of life. Consequently, in this work old age is not approached as a problem; instead, it is considered a challenge to be met by the development of programs. It is perhaps a challenge to all of us to articulate a series of desired social outcomes for older persons.

The book is divided into four parts. Part I is a review of major planning efforts that are currently ongoing. It moves from a macro to micro concept by first outlining federal planning strategies, then moving to a discussion of regional and state offices, and finally examining Title III programs at the multicounty level. The selections are by planners and program administrators representing these various agencies. Part II discusses direct services to the elderly by presenting a review via an academic point of view.

Part III attempts to respond to the increasing emphasis on volunteerism among the aged. the ACTION Program, one of the major sources for voluntary activities among older people, and the Retired Senior Volunteer Program, a very popular member of the ACTION family, are reviewed. An article discussing community responsibilities for providing volunteer opportunities follows. Part III concludes with a discussion of the role of volunteerism in contemporary society.

Part IV is developed from the ombudsman point of view. The advocacy program initiated by Citizens for Better Care in Michigan, the South Carolina Ombudsman Program, and the Michigan Ombudsman Program are described by personnel actively involved in these programs.

While this handbook will not provide complete information on the programs discussed, we hope it will at least serve as a beginning of knowledge.

Lorin A. Baumhover
Director, Center for the Study
of Aging, UNIVERSITY OF ALABAMA,
UNIVERSITY, ALABAMA

Joan Dechow Jones
Director, Gerontology Program,
ANTIOCH COLLEGE/COLUMBIA,
COLUMBIA, MARYLAND

PART I
Planning

1
FEDERAL STRATEGIES IN IMPLEMENTING AGING PROGRAMS

Joan Dechow Jones

This chapter reviews the development of Title III and Title VII of the Older Americans Act of 1965, the amendments to each title, and the most currently enacted Title III legislation.

Since Title III and Title VII were implemented in ways that made them mutually supportive, one cannot be discussed without mention of the other. Because Title III is directed toward planning while Title VII provides for direct social services, understanding these separate but interdependent titles presents a problem even to persons familiar with both programs. In order to facilitate this understanding, a chronological format is utilized.

The Older Americans Act was enacted on July 14, 1965, and stated that its goal was:

> To provide assistance in the development of new or improved programs to help older persons through grants to the states for community planning and services and for training, through research, development, or training project grants, and to establish within the Department of Health, Education, and Welfare an operating agency to be designated as the "Administration on Aging."[1]

Title I of the act contained the ten objectives that comprised the philosophical base of the 1965 law and all subsequent amendments. These objectives cut across major areas of federal programming and included:

(1) An adequate income in retirement in accordance with the American standard of living.
(2) The best possible physical and mental health which science can make available and without regard to economic status.
(3) Suitable housing, independently selected, designed and located

with reference to special needs and available at costs which older citizens can afford.

(4) Full restorative services for those who require institutional care.
(5) Opportunity for employment with no discriminatory personnel practices because of age.
(6) Retirement in health, honor, dignity—after years of contribution to the economy.
(7) Pursuit of meaningful activity within the widest range of civic, cultural, and recreational opportunities.
(8) Efficient community services, including access to low-cost transportation, which provide social assistance in a coordinated manner and which are readily available when needed.
(9) Immediate benefit from proven research knowledge which can sustain and improve health and happiness.
(10) Freedom, independence, and the free exercise of individual initiative in planning and managing their own lives. [2]

Section 201(a) of Title II established the Administration on Aging (AoA), the agency which administers all programs funded under the Older Americans Act of 1965 and subsequent amendments.

Title III

For the purpose of this discussion, the most important aspect of the Older Americans Act of 1965 is Title III. This title provided grants for community planning, services, and training. Its basic provisions supported community planning and coordination of programs, demonstrations of programs of activities, training of special personnel, and establishment of new or expansion of existing programs in such areas as recreational and other leisure-time activities, and informational, health, welfare, counseling, and referral services for older persons.

A proper understanding of the significance of this title requires an examination of its evolution and of the program strategies which the AoA utilized for implementing the title. Two strategies that were quite different in focus were developed:

(1) Strategy I: The AoA and the state agencies on aging as major service delivery agencies.
(2) Strategy II: Federal-state and substate focal points on aging.

Strategy I

Strategy I provided that the funds for state agencies on aging operations were, by law, a percentage of the amount they received for community grants.

This provision, which assured that a state agency would be created in each state, was a major step forward. However, since the operating funds were tapped from the community grants, it also assured that most states would treat the new state agency on aging as a very small operating unit rather than as a focal point on aging.

Because the states were not given a clear charter to serve as federal focal points and because it was difficult to make a "focal point role" work, a services delivery strategy was adopted. The AoA general counsel ruled that the law precluded the AoA from establishing priorities as to which services would be funded. Thus, the state agencies were expected to fund useful projects whose popularity would generate pressure from other locations for similar projects, with the result that there would be a rapid expansion of the program and large-scale funding. Based on this service delivery strategy, at its peak the original Title III program supported over 1,000 individual projects around the country.

The strategy was ultimately a failure, however, because of the interplay of a variety of factors:

(1) The costs of the Vietnam War began to make it harder to expand social program budgets.

(2) The advent of Robert McNamara's Planning, Programming, Budgeting System (PPBS) in the Department of Health, Education, and Welfare emphasized rational planning to justify program growth.

(3) The 1,000 state-funded projects could not be rationalized in terms of any prioritizing of most needed services or target groups, thereby hardening the opposition of the Office of Management and Budget to budget increases.

(4) Because the states had spread their monies very thinly, the projects, although each was sound individually, made little impact upon the community as a whole and did not generate a public demand for expansion, which would have moved Congress to raise the budget.

(5) The Title III budget never rose above $16 million.

As implemented in Title III of the Older Americans Act, the practice of funding numerous small projects throughout the country was not successful—either in generating increased public demand for more programs on the basis of successful model programs, or in generating additional money from the federal government for aging programs. By 1969, it seemed clear that Strategy I was stalemated. As a consequence, the AoA formulated the second strategy: federal-state and substate focal points on aging.

Strategy II

An analysis conducted by AoA led to the conclusion that their best chance for a funding breakthrough was the 1971 White House Conference on Aging, which was to be held close to the 1972 presidential election year. Title III as amended in 1969 gave the AoA the authority to fund a variety of Areawide Model Projects on a demonstration project grant basis. The pertinent amendment read, in part, as follows:

> Sec. 305. (a) The Secretary is authorized . . . to make grants to or contracts with State agencies . . . [for] the development and operation of statewide, regional, metropolitan area, county, city, or other areawide model projects for carrying out the purposes of this title. [3]

These projects were to test a variety of approaches to achieving coordination between existing public and private service agencies serving the elderly; to prioritize service gaps; and to obtain new funds to fill the priority gaps.

The AoA intended that the Areawide Model Projects funded in 1969 would provide an experiential base for completely revising Title III when it came up for renewal in 1972. Their rationale was that, with three years' experience, they would be in a good position to capitalize on the momentum built up by the 1971 White House Conference. However, the timetable did not work out exactly as planned: the Office of Management and Budget funded the projects toward the end of the *1971* fiscal year, and not in 1970 as had been hoped. Therefore, the experience that was to be a basis for writing the new Title III law turned out to be quite limited.

1973 Amendments

In the 1973 amendments to the Older Americans Act, Section 301 completely revised Title III, although there was no change in the title heading, which read "Title III—Grants for Community Planning, Services, and Training." Section 301 indicated the purpose of the new Title III:

> Sec. 301. It is the purpose of this title to encourage and assist State and local agencies to concentrate resources in order to develop greater capacity and foster the development of comprehensive and coordinated service systems to serve older persons by entering into new cooperative arrangements with each other and with providers of social services for planning for the provision of, and providing social services and, where necessary, to reorganize or reassign functions. [4]

As amended in 1973, Section 304 imposed the following AoA requirements on state organizations wishing to qualify for Title III funds:

> (1) The State shall, in accordance with regulations of the Commissioner, designate a State agency as the sole State agency to: (a) develop the State plan to be submitted to the Commissioner for

approval, (b) administer the State plan within such State, (c) be primarily responsible for the coordination of all state activities related to the purpose of this Act, (d) review and comment, at the request of any Federal department or agency, any application from any agency or organization within such State to such Federal department or agency for assistance; and (e) divide the entire State into distinct areas in accordance with regulations of the Commissioner.

(2) The State agency designated pursuant to (1) shall—determine for which planning and service areas an area plan will be developed; and . . . [designate area agencies on aging which must be] any office or agency of a unit of general purpose local government, which is designated for this purpose by the chief elected official or officials of such unit.[5]

In order to be approved by the state agency, a proposed area agency on aging was directed to develop an area plan for planning and service which would:

(1) provide for the establishment of a comprehensive and coordinated system for the delivery of social services within the planning and service area covered by the plan;

(2) . . . provide for the initiation, expansion, or improvement of social services in the planning and service area covered by the area plan;

(3) provide for the establishment or maintenance of information and referral sources in sufficient numbers to assure that all older persons within the planning and service area covered by the plan will have reasonably convenient access to such sources.[6]

In addition, the area agency was directed to "conduct periodic evaluations of activities carried out pursuant to the area plan." The area agency on aging was, therefore, legally required to conduct evaluations of any social services planned and/or delivered in respective areas. In the 1973 amendments, Title III clearly focused on the planning and coordination of services to the elderly rather than on direct service delivery. The 1973 Title III law provided for the establishment of area agencies on aging within already recognized local units of government. It required each designated area agency to develop a comprehensive and coordinated system for planning, coordinating, and pooling resources; for providing information and, when feasible, contracting for the delivery of services; and for evaluating the effectiveness and efficiency of the service delivery system.

Title VII Background

The 1972 amendments to the Older Americans Act inserted Title VII, a national nutrition program for older Americans. It had its roots in a number of pilot programs begun in 1968 under Title VI of the act, in accordance with congressional directives. These programs demonstrated a very real need for nutrition projects for older persons, both to improve their diet and to engage them in the process of socialization—drawing them out of the isolation in which so many confined themselves and making available ancillary services such as health, recreation, and social services.

Congress enacted a permanent program based on the pilot projects, and President Richard Nixon signed it into law on March 22, 1972. This legislation (Title VII) authorized the AoA to allocate funds to the states for the establishment of central accessible locations at which persons sixty years of age or older and their spouses could receive hot nutritious meals at least five days a week. [7]

Funds for this program were authorized to be appropriated for the fiscal year 1973-1974. Unfortunately, President Nixon vetoed bills appropriating funds for the new programs, thereby preventing their getting underway in fiscal 1973 as anticipated by the legislation. Funds in the amount of $100 million were finally appropriated at the end of fiscal 1973, to be available on December 31, 1973. For fiscal 1974, $104 million were appropriated.

Section 705 of Title VII related to the administration of this program within the states and required that a single state agency be established to administer this program. It was further required that the Title VII plan be coordinated with the state plan and with other agencies providing social services in the planning area. Section 705 also required any state funded under Title VII to submit to the state unit on aging a state plan that was to be coordinated with Section 304 (Title III) of the Older Americans Act, which provided for the establishment of area plans of action. As a result of this requirement, the AoA made *coordination mandatory between Title III, which funded area agencies on aging, and Title VII, which provided for direct service delivery.*

Requirements

Section 706(a) of the Older Americans Act, as amended in 1972, described the program requirements for the Title VII nutritional program.

Nutrition projects were to be established which, five or more days per week, would provide at least one hot meal per day, assuring a minimum of one-third of the daily recommended dietary allowance. Open to individuals sixty years of age or over and their spouses, the nutrition projects were to be located in areas close to the older people's homes. In addition, they were to develop outreach programs to seek out older people who might wish to participate. Recreational activities, information and referral services, and health and welfare counseling were also to be made available at each nutrition site.

The manual of policies and procedures which the Department of Health, Education, and Welfare distributed to states implementing Title VII programs required that the following supporting social services be instituted: outreach, transportation, personal escort, information and referral, health and welfare counseling, nutrition education, shopping assistance, and recreation incidental to the project.

Accomplishments

The funding delays resulting from the presidential vetoes in 1973 created severe handicaps for the program. Potential state and local recipients of grants under the nutritional legislation were understandably unwilling to commit themselves and their local resources until the federal government matched promises with hard money. Hence, despite the long lead time between passage of the legislation in March 1972 and the allocation of the first funds to the states on July 27, 1973, little preparatory work was done at state and local levels during this period. The funds finally allocated were not made available to the states for making grants to local nutrition projects until December 31, 1973. At this point, a rather chaotic scramble ensued in which the states began to prepare and submit plans to the AoA, and project applicants approached the state agencies. Sites had to be found, staffs employed, arrangements made for food preparation, outreach begun, and a host of other details attended to.

To facilitate the implementation of the programs, Dr. Arthur Flemming, the commissioner on aging, suspended the requirements for the eight supportive services for ninety days. When that period was up, upon the recommendation of the states and with the approval of the AoA, the requirements were suspended for an additional ninety days. [8] This action permitted nutritional projects to concentrate on the preparation and delivery of food at congregate sites. In many cases, however, suspension of the supportive services requirements meant the total suspension of much needed social services which would have kept the nutrition program from being classified as a free meals or give-away program. By December 31, 1973, each of the states had completed its allocation of $99 million to 665 nutrition projects across the country.

By February 1, 1974, the AoA's weekly report demonstrated that 80,000 meals were being served each day to Americans aged sixty and older. By March 31, Commissioner Flemming stated that 200,000 meals were being served daily and that the figure would increase to an estimated 212,000 meals a day by the end of 1974. AoA statistics also indicated that 70 percent of the meals were being served to persons below the poverty threshold and that 37 percent of the recipients were members of minority groups. [9]

Extension of Title VII

On October 25, 1973, H.R. 11105, a bill to extend nutrition programs for the elderly for three years, was introduced. H.R. 11105 authorized $150 million for fiscal year 1975, $175 million for fiscal 1976, and $200 million for fiscal 1977 for programs supported under Title VII.

On February 13 and 14, 1974, the Subcommittee on Select Education of the Committee on Education and Labor held hearings on H.R. 11105 and related measures. The testimony not only overwhelmingly favored extending the nutritional program for the elderly, but also supported extending the amounts authorized to be appropriated.

On February 20, 1974, the subcommittee amended the bill to authorize appropriations of $150 million for fiscal 1975, $200 million for fiscal 1976, and $250 million for fiscal 1977, and reported the bill as amended by unanimous vote.

Recent Amendments to the Older Americans Act Relating to Title III

During January and February 1975, Congressman John Brademas of Indiana held hearings relating to Title III of the Older Americans Act. Commissioner Flemming testified that during 1974 state agencies concentrated on the establishment of state advisory committees on aging (which created 412 area agencies on aging covering 70 percent of the older population nationally) and/or the development of information and referral sources. In addition to these efforts, the state agencies had also been active in assisting older persons with problems related to the energy crisis and unemployment.

Testimony taken at the hearings indicated that Title III had established area agencies in order to make resources and services available for older persons in their immediate communities in a central location. The majority of the 412 area agencies established in 1974 were located within city and county governments, or within regional councils of governments. Forty-seven percent were located in rural areas and 53 percent in urban areas. In fiscal year 1974, $68 million were appropriated for carrying out the programs for the elderly through the area agencies on aging.

Although much of the testimony before the Subcommittee on Select Education endorsed the area agency concept, there had been little time before the hearings to develop empirical documentation on the effectiveness of area agencies on aging. Indeed, during the hearings, many of the House members of the committee indicated they lacked sufficient information on the area agency concept and were therefore unable to determine its possible effectiveness on the local level.

Current Strategy

In hearings during January and February 1975, before a subcommittee of the Committee on Education and Welfare in the House, Commissioner Flemming outlined the basic operational strategies of the AoA for fiscal 1976. In recapping the 1973 and 1974 amendments to the Older Americans Act, Flemming pointed out that these changes had provided the basis for installing and operating a nationwide network on aging. Whereas in fiscal 1974 the AoA had placed primary emphasis on installation, now attention would be given to operate the network in such a manner "as to make a significant contribution to serving the needs of today's older persons." [10]

With the maintenance of this important network in mind, Flemming outlined the priorities of the AoA:

1. *The process of coordinating the resources made available under the Older Americans Act with other public and private resources is for the delivery of services to older persons.*
These coordinated resources were to take place as directed by Section 301 of the act. Specifically, state and area agencies were called on to enter into new cooperative agreements with each other and to provide comprehensive and coordinated services on behalf of older persons.

2. *A high priority has been given during fiscal year 1975 to working out and implementing interagency agreements.*
Flemming noted that in 1974 the interagency agreement was used to develop formal working agreements with a number of agencies both inside and outside the Department of Health, Education, and Welfare.

In facilitating the state and area agencies' power to make cooperative agreements, the AoA has made some such agreements on the federal level. Some of these include:

1. *Transportation*—Department of Transportation
2. *Utilization of Volunteers*—ACTION
3. *Information and Referral*—Social Security Administration, Social Rehabilitative Services
4. *Medicaid Services*—Medical Services Administration
5. *Rehabilitation Services*—Rehabilitation Services Administration
6. *Health Services*—Public Health Service
7. *Use of School Buses for the Elderly*—Department of Transportation, Office of Education
8. *Housing*—Department of Housing and Urban Development
9. *Coordination of School Lunch Programs and Facilities*—Office of Education
10. *Energy*—Departments of Agriculture, Labor, and Housing and Urban Development, Federal Energy Administration, Community Services Administration, ACTION
11. *Housing and Nutrition*—Department of Housing and Urban Development [11]

In his testimony, Flemming also pointed out that the process of providing the state and area agencies with maximum opportunity to respond to the priority needs of older persons within their jurisdiction would be maintained. Thus, the autonomy of state and area agencies in dealing with their own aging constituents would be assured, despite certain commitments between federal agencies at the national level.

Micro to Macro

In the development of Titles III and VII of Older Americans Act, the AoA progressed from a micro to a macro point of view. In the early stages of program implementation, the micro viewpoint was adopted. The AoA's first implementation strategy was to sponsor many small direct service programs throughout the country in the hopes that such programs would create a demand for additional services. This strategy could have been successful. After the White House Conference on Aging in 1971, Strategy II was adopted to delineate state and substate units on aging. This strategy of establishing area agencies on aging as substate planning units was successfully implemented in 1973. It was placed on firmer foundation in 1974 as more and more states qualified for Title III funds and established area agencies on aging within units of local government. The most current strategy, following the successful implementation of the area agency concept, is to negotiate cooperative agreements with agencies on a federal level to provide a foundation for such agreements on state and substate levels. This effort is designed to maximize the planning, coordination, and pooling of resources as required for area agencies.

By making agreements at the national level, the AoA intended to provide a national framework for serving the needs of elderly people throughout the United States. It remains for state and local governments to take advantage of these agreements. In this way, opportunity is provided at the federal level while autonomy rests with the state and substate units on aging. Whether this strategy will be successful will be determined by the success of cooperative agreements at the state level during the 1977-1978 fiscal year.

Notes

1. U.S. Department of Health, Education, and Welfare, *Older Americans Act of 1965, as Amended, and Related Acts* (Washington, D.C.: U.S. Government Printing Office, December 1974), p. 1.

2. Ibid., pp. 2-3.

3. U.S. Congress, *To Amend the Older Americans Act of 1965, Statutes of 1965, Statutes at Large.* 94th Cong., 1st sess., 1975.

4. *Older Americans Act of 1965, as Amended*, pp. 13-14.

5. Ibid., p. 19.

6. Ibid., p. 20.

7. Ibid., p. 43.

8. Dr. Arthur Flemming, Information Memorandum AoA-IM-73-62, October 1973, Washington, D.C.

9. *Hearings before the Subcommittee on Aging of the Committee on Labor and Public Welfare on S. 2488, S. 3100, S. 3195, and H.R. 11105*, Legislation amending and extending nutrition programs for the elderly, 93d Cong., 2d sess., 1974, pp. 182-226.

10. *Hearings before the Subcommittee on Select Education of the Committee on Education and Labor* on P.L. 93-29, 94th Cong, 1st sess., 1975, p. 83.

11. Ibid., pp. 84-85.

2
REGIONAL OFFICES OF AGING

Willis Atwell

Regional offices of aging are located in each of ten regions which conform to the boundaries set up by the Department of Health, Education, and Welfare. The following is the list of regions, locations of regional offices, and the states served by each:

Region I—Boston: Connecticut, Maine, Massachusetts, New Hampshire, Rhode Island, Vermont

Region II—New York: New Jersey, New York, Puerto Rico, Virgin Islands

Region III—Philadelphia: Delaware, District of Columbia, Maryland, Pennsylvania, Virginia, West Virginia

Region IV—Atlanta: Alabama, Florida, Georgia, Kentucky, Mississippi, North Carolina, South Carolina, Tennessee

Region V—Chicago: Illinois, Indiana, Michigan, Minnesota, Ohio, Wisconsin

Region VI—Dallas: Arkansas, Louisiana, New Mexico, Oklahoma, Texas

Region VII—Kansas City: Iowa, Kansas, Missouri, Nebraska

Region VIII—Denver: Colorado, Montana, North Dakota, South Dakota, Utah, Wyoming

Region IX—San Francisco: Arizona, California, Guam, Hawaii, Nevada, Samoa, Trust Territory

Region X—Seattle: Alaska, Idaho, Oregon, Washington

Authorization and Functions of Regional Directors

The regional offices of the Department of Health, Education, and Welfare were established under the Office of the Secretary by the Congress. The regional director in each of the HEW regions officially represents the secretary and reports to the secretary and under secretary. The regional director's office coordinates HEW's programs and activities within the region, and represents the department in official dealings with state and other governmental units, representatives of Congress, and the general public.

Regional office functions or planned revisions are announced by official publication in the *Federal Register*. Such publications of intentions give the Congress, the executive branch, and the public an opportunity to know what official actions are taking place and to enter objections if they so desire. Practitioners in the field of aging are perhaps more familiar with publication of notices in the *Federal Register* to establish or amend federal regulations, such as those covering Title III and Title VII of the Older Americans Act, as amended.

An example of this procedure with respect to regional offices appeared in a recent issue of the *Federal Register* (Vol. 40, No. 6, January 9, 1975, pp. 1726-1731). The publication listed the organization, functions, and delegation of authority for the regional director in Region VII, Kansas City. The notice detailed such functions as developing regional priorities, formulating plans for each priority and assuring that regional agency heads achieve all their objectives in accordance with their plans. In addition, the regional director develops continuing cooperative relationships with officials of federal agencies in the region; uses regional councils to insure that interdepartmental delivery of services can be more effective; administers child development programs in the region and makes certain Head Start grants; develops plans for emergency preparedness and maintains a written plan for regional emergency operations, including emergencies and natural disasters under the Disaster Relief Act of 1974; and through the Office of Long Term Care Standards Enforcement, administers activities related to the approval and termination of agreements with skilled nursing facilities in either Medicare or in both Medicare and Medicaid programs. Each regional director has other specific duties, but these have the most direct bearing on his activities.

Each of the ten regional directors is in charge of his particular regional office and its component parts, including the regional office for human development and the office of aging. The director of the office of aging reports to the commissioner for aging and, by extension, to the central office program units. In addition, the director of the office of aging reports to the regional director for human development. The staff responsible for aging programs in the regional offices occupies positions (or "slots" as termed by the government) as allocated to the Administration on Aging. Hence, the director of the office of aging has a dual responsibility, both to the central office and to the regional office. In order to maintain central and regional office relationships on as balanced a basis as possible, the commissioner has, as part of his office, the field liaison staff. A comparable function for the assistant secretary for human development is carried out by the regional office specialist.

Delegation of Authority

One of the functions of the regional director is that of administering child development programs in the region. This program is included here to point out some differences between the directors of the offices of aging and of the other regional program units. The directors of the offices of aging, for example, are limited by congressional action and do not have the granting authority belonging to some other regional program units, such as the regional Office of Child Development (OCD). The regional OCD director makes grants directly, under the authority delegated to the regional director and under line authority to the assistant regional director for human development and the director of child development. The key word in the previous sentence is "delegated." Delegation of this kind of authority is prohibited to the director of the office of aging by law. The Older Americans Act, as amended, Title II, Section 201, states:

> There is established in the Office of the Secretary an Administration on Aging which shall be headed by a Commissioner on Aging. Except for Title VI and as otherwise specifically provided by the Older Americans Comprehensive Services Amendments of 1973, the Administration shall be the principle agency for carrying out this Act. In the performance of his functions, the Commissioner shall be directly responsible to the Office of the Secretary. *The Secretary shall not approve any delegation of the functions of the Commissioner to any other officer not directly responsible to the Commissioner.* [Author's italics.]

Thus, the directors of the regional offices of aging are prevented from handling directly the Title IV-A discretionary grants for training programs under the sponsorship of state agencies on aging, institutions of higher learning, other educational institutions, and public or private nonprofit organizations or agencies. Regional offices normally work with such institutions and agencies in their general activities.

In helping to implement the Title III and Title VII programs under the Older Americans Act, as amended, the regional offices of aging act both as extensions of the commissioner and central office program units and as professionals providing technical assistance directly to the state agencies on aging and, through them, to the area agencies on aging and the Title VII nutrition projects. Technical assistance ranges from interpretation of federal regulations to training state staff in such areas as setting objectives under the Operational

Planning System. However, the principal functions of the regional offices with regard to Title III and Title VII are to process state plans and to regularly monitor and assess state operations.

State Plan

Although the AoA has generally made some modifications from year to year in the state plan format and requirements, the basic requirements remain the same. The following is a summary of the state plan for fiscal year 1976, under which states are currently operating:

Part I—Objectives: This part has two major sections: (1) a summary listing of state objectives, and (2) a statement of state objectives for Title III and Title VII, including the rationale and action steps for each objective.

Part II—Action Plans: This segment groups all of the elements related to fundamental aspects of the state agency's capacity to further develop the Title III and Title VII programs. Included are action plans for technical assistance; assessment; coordination; information and referral sources; involvement of state advisory committees, advisory councils of area agencies, and nutrition project councils; increasing participation of low-income and minority older persons; grants and contracts to minority agencies and organizations; equal employment opportunity; and training and manpower development.

Part III—Resource Allocation Plans: All of the fiscal data relative to the state plan are brought together in this part. These include the summary resource allocation plan, followed respectively by the Title III and Title VII resource allocation plans.

Part IV—General Provisions: This part brings together all materials relating to the organizational and administrative aspects of the state agency; information on the state advisory committee; materials on planning and service areas; and older population characteristics.

Part V—Supplemental Exhibits: The final part of the plan format consists of three supplemental exhibits concerning a modified definition of low income, direct provision of social services by the state agency, and demonstration projects of statewide significance. In addition, there is a special supplement to the standard state plan format for a state that requests designation as a single state planning and service area.

This summary demonstrates that the preparation of the state plan is a major undertaking; indeed, several months intervene between the issuance of its format and the submittal of the final document. During this period, the regional staff works with the state staff in its preparation, reviewing the requirements, overseeing the development of materials for the various sections, assuring that the mutually agreed timetable is being followed, and attending at least some of the required public hearings. Once the state plan has been completed, the regional office of aging makes recommendations to the commissioner for approval; for approval with specified conditions; or for revisions. In making its recommendations, the regional office furnishes a letter which is addressed to the governor, and is for the commissioner's signature.

The Monitoring and Assessment Process

Based on the state plan, the regional office regularly monitors and assesses the state's progress in implementing its plan. Although the commissioner prefers to make monthly visits to state agencies to provide technical assistance on their operations and programming, at least two-day, quarterly on-site visits are required. During the course of the year, regional offices are required to complete the prescribed monitoring and assessment process. The process that regional offices use with the state agencies covers the following areas of interest:

I. *State Agency Administration*: This section covers the location of the state agency in state government; organizational structure; legal authority; staffing; advisory committee activities; and technical assistance to area agencies and Title II nutrition projects, including administration recordkeeping, accounting, staffing, and programming.

II. *Planning*: This area includes the development of state objectives and their accomplishment or problems in implementation; analysis of special needs of the populations to be served; special studies on the needs of older persons and plans for meeting their needs; the collection of data as a basis for developing plans to meet the needs of the target populations; and the establishment and use of the hearings system to provide consumer involvement and viewpoints.

III. *Coordination/Pooling*: Since much of the success of coordination and pooling mandated by the Congress in the Older Americans Act, as amended, depends on working agreements and public information, these are covered in some detail. Although the AoA now has seventeen interagency agreements which it encourages state agencies to implement, only those covering information and referral and Title XX of the Social Security Act are required to be implemented by the state agencies on aging. The importance of a strong public information program is obvious in the ongoing program of the state agency.

IV. *Evaluation*: The state agency is required to have an action plan covering its own evaluation and monitoring of administration and management of grants and contracts. In addition, mandatory evaluations are conducted on area agencies and Title VII nutrition projects.

V. *Information and Referral*: The 1973 amendments to the Older Americans Act required older persons to have reasonably convenient and accessible sources of information and referral services by the end of fiscal 1975. Guidelines covering minimum requirements, along with guides toward setting up a more comprehensive system, were issued. The regional office strives to exceed minimum standards and therefore makes continuous efforts to improve information and referral services.

VI. *Planning and Service Areas*: The first step in the implementation of area agencies in the 1973 amendments to the Older Americans Act was the division of the state by the governor into planning and service areas. Although some states immediately converted all designated planning and service areas to area agencies on aging, others decided to concentrate their resources on those area agencies serving the majority of the states' older population. Therefore, this section of the assessment also covers the development of the unconverted planning and service areas, as planned by the state.

VII. *Area Agencies on Aging*: This important section of the assessment covers the development of area agencies in accordance with the Older Americans Act and federal regulations.

VIII. *Nutrition Projects*: This is also a key area and covers the Title VII nutrition projects in terms of legislation and federal regulations, making sure that the required number of meals are served, that the people being served meet the eligibility criteria, that minority contractors are used, that prescribed social services are in place, that project councils are operating, and that other requirements have been met.

IX. *Projects Not Under Area Plans*: Existing legislation provides that some projects (other than area agencies and Title VII nutrition projects) be funded by the state agency on aging in those sections of the state not covered by area plans. As a result, the AoA through the regional offices must also assess these projects to insure they conform to requirements.

X. *Fiscal Administration and Management*: The regional offices are responsible for seeing that state agencies maintain fiscal accountability in line with federal requirements, that the accounting system is adequate and facilitates effective budget administration, and that procurement standards conform to legal requirements. Other responsibilities are a review of the state agency's grant awards procedures, recordkeeping and reporting, documentation of the matching of nonfederal for federal funding, maintenance of property management policies and procedures, and an internal audit plan in line with accepted auditing procedures.

XI. *General*: This action covers such matters as the maintenance of effort, a term meaning that each recipient of an award is expending the same amount of funds as in the previous year and is complying with the approved civil rights procedures.

In addition to assessing state agencies in these areas, the regional offices review the similar assessments that state agencies on aging make of their area agencies and Title VII nutrition projects. They are also on call to accompany state agency staff in their on-site assessment visits. From the scope of the assessment and monitoring process, it is evident that the regional office staff must be conversant with existing legislation, central office memoranda and issuances, and other federal regulations and requirements. Some knowledge of adequate recordkeeping and grants management procedures is also required. Since some of these areas of concern involve highly technical materials, the regional office staff makes arrangements for assistance from the grants management staff of the regional office for human development, the regional Civil Service Commission staff, civil rights officials, and other personnel available in the regional offices.

The Operational Planning System

The regional offices report regularly to the Operational Planning System (OPS) on such activities as the assessment and monitoring of state agencies on aging. The OPS is a tool that allows every level of management to effectively handle program activities and monitor progress toward their achievement. In the event there are difficulties preventing such progress, problems may be analyzed and effective decisions regarding the resolution of the difficulties may be made. Some goals of the OPS are jointly agreed upon by the assistant secretary for human development and the commissioner and involve both the central office and regional offices. These goals become primary objectives on which both regional and central offices report through the commissioner to the assistant secretary at monthly management meetings. In addition, both the regional director and assistant regional director for human development may have objectives affecting the regional offices of aging; these objectives are reviewed at monthly management meetings along with the primary objectives established by the assistant secretary.

Failure to achieve any of the activities related to the regional or primary objectives must be explained to the responsible managers, and new dates for their accomplishment must be negotiated. Similarly, central office failures must be reported to the assistant secretary and to the regional officials as justification for regional offices not being able to accomplish their activities. It was anticipated that in fiscal 1976 regional offices would spend at least 80 percent of their time on achieving the objectives defined by the commissioner and assistant secretary. These objectives relate directly to the achievement of action steps based on the legislative requirements of the Older Americans Act, as amended.

A number of regional offices are working with state agencies on aging to develop objectives derived from the state plan and are utilizing the management conference as a tool to monitor and assess state agency progress. Similarly, state agencies are instituting this management tool in order to keep abreast of area agency progress toward their plans stated in terms of objectives and action steps. Technical assistance materials for setting up and monitoring objectives were issued by the AoA.

The leadership of the regional director is important in developing continuing cooperative relationships with officials of other federal agencies in the region and in the work of the Federal Regional Councils (FRC). In implementing interagency agreements initiated by the commissioner on aging, the offices of aging have a considerable responsibility for effecting relationships with counterpart federal officials and then jointly bringing about state agreements between these counterparts. Some regional directors have provided support through the FRC committee on aging, while others have developed interagency ad hoc committees to implement the agreements. Some have also written letters to the governors concerning the importance of agreements. The accountability of the offices of aging for implementing agreements is included in the OPS objectives. In addition, the commissioner receives regular monthly reports from central office staff members who maintain regular telephone communication with designated regional office staff members.

"Hot Line"

The commissioner has established a "hot line" relationship between the field liaison staff at headquarters and the regional offices of aging on disaster-related activities or whenever older persons are disaster victims. In presidentially declared disasters, the HEW network is immediately activated. Because regional directors are officially involved in emergency preparedness and disaster activities under the Disaster Relief Act of 1974, the offices of aging are given recognition and support in their efforts on behalf of elderly disaster victims. As in other AoA programs, the office of aging staff works with the state agency on aging and the area agencies in the affected area. The AoA is developing a series of working agreements with agencies and organizations to insure their full cooperation in meeting the special postdisaster needs of older persons.

Voluntary Groups

Under the 1973 amendments to the Older Americans Act, the commissioner is directed to encourage and permit voluntary groups to participate in AoA programs for older persons. This responsibility is shared by the regional offices of aging, which work closely with available representatives of national organizations with whom the commissioner meets regularly. For example, the commissioner meets regularly with the National Association of State Units on Aging, the Urban Elderly Coalition representing the directors of aging programs in large cities, and the national organization representing AAAs, all of which are funded under the Older Americans Act; and with key officials of the national organizations representing concerns of older persons—the American Association of Retired Persons/National Retired Teachers Association, the National Association of Retired Federal Employees, the National Council on Aging, and the National Council of Senior Citizens, all of which are grantees of the Department of Labor under Title IX of the Older Americans Act. The commissioner also meets with the National Caucus for the Black Aged and, in some cases, with representatives from the American National Red Cross, AFL-CIO, and the National Urban League.

Regional offices of aging often assist organizations and special interest groups holding research, demonstration, or training grants from the AoA. The regional staff on aging also participates in professional organizations, such as the Gerontological Society and the Association for Gerontology in Higher Education, and in professional conferences.

Long-Term Care

The regional director's responsibility for activities related to the termination of agreements with skilled nursing facilities also directly involves the directors of the offices of aging. In late 1973, the under secretary transferred to the AoA the responsibility for taking "the lead in implementing a coordinated program for assuring that alternative arrangements are made for those displaced from sub-standard nursing homes"; "for implementing a coordinated program for protecting private individuals when they purchase nursing home services"; for overseeing "the Department's program to stimulate development of nursing home ombudsman programs in the States"; for implementing a short-term strategy "for utilizing alternatives to nursing homes where quality of medical care is not a primary consideration"; and for ensuring that programs developed by state and area agencies "to meet the needs of persons living in their own homes are also used to meet the comparable needs of persons living in nursing homes."

Ombudsman and Other Alternatives

In carrying out these responsibilities, the commissioner has funded, in each state agency, a nursing home ombudsman developmental specialist whose activities are monitored by the regional office staff on aging. In addition, some regional offices of aging have worked with regional committees on aging in developing alternatives to institutionalization. Others have worked with state agencies to develop relocation plans for nursing home patients; some of these plans could handle nursing home closings resulting from the termination of agreements by the regional director or from the effects of natural disasters.

The regional staff also serves as the link with the headquarters' public information unit providing material for AGING magazine on unusual or innovative programs in state or in area agencies on aging. Conversely, it also secures literature and pamphlets for meetings, state aging conferences, or special programs during Older Americans Month in May. The commissioner calls on the regional staff to participate in developing policy and program materials in cooperation with the central office staff. The purpose of such joint activities is to provide the broadest possible viewpoint. Regional directors meet quarterly with the commissioner, and the commissioner or a member of the executive staff meets quarterly with each regional staff.

Other Functions

The regional directors of the offices of aging and staff members have various duties and functions. For example, any letters relating to aging that are addressed to the regional director by members of Congress, state officials, or the public may require drafting help from the unit on aging. The staff on aging may also be tapped by the regional director or assistant regional directors for various assignments on task forces, study groups, or committees. The regional directors of the offices of aging are responsible for directing the staff on aging, maintaining desirable levels of performance, meeting the responsibilities assigned by the regional director and his subordinates and by the commissioner and his headquarters' units, as well as meeting the needs of the state agencies on aging for assistance and encouragement. The organization of the director's staff varies from region to region. Some staffs are organized by units responsible for programmatic or functional activities and by geographical responsibility, each with a deputy director; some have combined programmatic/functional and geographical responsibilities; and others are organized along variations of these two staffing patterns.

Positions

A total of 127 positions are allocated to the offices of aging in the ten regions. Most of the directors have been with the program on aging for several years and thus have a grasp of the historical development of the aging program. This is perhaps one reason why in a period of ten years the AoA has progressed from a rather simple federal-state program to a complex national network on aging.

3
PLANNING IN STATE AGENCIES ON AGING

Phillip L. Nathanson

The passage of the 1973 amendments to the Older Americans Act of 1965 changed the entire thrust of funding mechanisms for Title III, the direct service grant program of the act. Its scope is now very broad, and most services for the elderly may be funded under it. Thus, the 1973 amendments significantly altered the role of state agencies on aging. Prior to 1973, the state agencies directly funded service organizations. With the establishment of the area agencies on aging (AAA) concept, the state agency has become an administrative body which funds another administrative body (AAA), which in turn funds the programs. In some cases, the state agency under Title VII directly funds the congregate meal program.

Each year the AAAs have become the administrative agent for a greater and greater proportion of the Title VII programs. This is not an undesirable situation, for it has resulted in more joint funding and a broader base of program planning.

Planning Components

The system will probably not tolerate two obviously administrative bodies funneling money and not providing direct service unless the state agency begins to concentrate on statewide issues. Such statewide issues include strategies for funding, information and referral systems, legislation, and service programs.

In order to produce competent planning, the state agency must have the following skills:

Program Skills: The state agency staff (particularly the planner) must have knowledge about how programs operate, including knowledge of boards of directors; staff-hiring procedures; service delivery; funding structures of agencies; interrelationships of communities, cities, counties, state, and federal agencies, and programs; and phases of organizational development from the inception of an organization to its bureaucratization.

Strategical Skills: The state agency must have an ongoing mechanism that establishes and adjusts priorities on a statewide basis. In many circles, this is known as a plan of action. A plan of action is necessary to maintain the state agency's focus. The strategy of a state agency should take into account the realities of a situation as well as some idealistic thought and desired outcomes. A distinction, then, needs to be made between what things are and what things should be. The state agencies should establish both goals and objectives and strive to meet them. Some state agencies actually attempt to meet goals while others merely attempt to survive. Although survival is a goal, it certainly is neither idealistic nor necessarily beneficial to older persons.

Organizing Skills: The state agency on aging is responsible for providing statewide leadership in the field of aging. Various organizations, such as area agencies on aging, and direct service providers have geographic boundaries. The state agency is frequently the only agency on the state level responsible for statewide coordination. Organizing is necessary to accomplish this function as well as to call statewide meetings with all Title VII nutrition directors, meet with all colleges and universities regarding aging and with all the nursing home administrators, distribute information about legislation, present statewide funding concepts, and explain new federal requirements.

Fund-Raising Skills: State units on aging usually do not attempt to provide funds other than those granted by the federal government. Money is constantly flowing from the federal government, and various monies are made available from different departments within the federal government. The state agency should inform its constituency of the availability of funds. In some cases, however, state agency administrators are reluctant to take on this additional burden, for they are unable to keep up with the volume of work that passes through their offices. If there is a statewide strategy for service delivery and its mechanisms, the state agency must find the funds to implement the strategy. Title III and state funds are insufficient to accomplish a broad-based strategy that will improve the quality of life for older persons. If the state agency does not implement a statewide strategy and is not seeking or has not secured funds for its implementation, then the state is not doing comprehensive planning.

Knowledge of the Data: The state agency should be collecting information in several areas:

1. Unmet needs
2. Needs that are being met
3. A current listing of agencies and organizations serving the elderly
4. The establishment of or use of an existing library
5. A list of political "influentials"

In addition to collecting information, the state agency should know what information it should *not* collect. Excessive collection of data makes it much more difficult to weed out irrelevant information. Those state agencies that overcollect are frequently seen as paper machines, baffling their audiences by the pounds of paper they generate.

Identifying the Planning Process of State Agencies

In assessing *how* the state agency is planning, it may be helpful to ask three questions:

1. *What is the decision-making process?* Undoubtedly, the most important question to answer is, "How are decisions made?" Are day-to-day decisions based on goals established by the agency (if, in fact, any real goals have been established)? Does the state agency have a work plan, and are decisions based upon the work plan? Probably one of the most important decision-making processes is that of how funds are distributed: some grants are funded arbitrarily, some are based on need, while others, as is all too common, are based on power politics. It is important to assess how much input the staff contributes to decision-making. If the staff and the community participate in the agency's decisions, then at least there is a rudimentary foundation on which a planning process can be built. Planning cannot be done by a single individual making decisions. Rather, good planning consists of a consensus process that establishes goals and objectives. The state agency that is exclusionary rather than inclusionary is probably not engaged in a good planning process. When planning has been accomplished, power and control become much less an issue; therefore, an inclusionary process is perhaps less threatening.

2. *What is the communication process?* The state agency's communications system is part of its planning process. It is assumed that state agency planning involves more than merely plotting a course of what needs to be accomplished. Comprehensive planning is a process that sets ideas into motion and is far more than a paper and pencil exercise. If, in fact, the scope of the state agency is statewide, then the communications system must be statewide in order to implement its planning and decision-making. When a particular action is needed, there must be a mechanism that will provide for feedback (input). If a state agency has been provided with a particular block of money, the state agency's constituents must be told what the money is for and to whom it is available. Without a good communications system, it is often difficult to reach most of those who are eligible for the money. Planning is not something to do *to* people, but rather *with* people.

3. *Has the state agency established some formal mechanism to document and collect met and unmet needs?* Does the state agency have a centralized data collection system? If it is doing proper planning, the state agency should distinguish between needs and wants. Often a group of older persons say they *need* something, when in fact, they are stating a *want*. For instance, the elderly may want recreation, when in fact, they have serious medical or dental needs

that are threatening their very lives. Generally, in these cases, wants are based on emotional needs while even greater and more immediate needs are necessary to continue functioning. The state agency should, to the greatest extent possible, be able to satisfy both their wants and needs. But in times of scarce resources, needs must be given priority over wants. A good balance in the use of resources for the elderly is, in part, a balance between what they need and what they want.

One major problem, then, with data collection instruments is distinguishing between what people need and what people want. Complicating the problem is the possibility that, in an interview, older people will tell the interviewer what it is he or she wants to hear. The older person is, in a sense, expressing what they want and not what they need: they may want the interviewer to come back, or their responses may reflect their efforts to preserve their pride and dignity. Most people find it easier to describe what they want and do not focus on growth needs. However, if the data collection instrument is carefully designed and is based on cognition and planning, it will be possible to distinguish between wants and needs. In plotting its course, the state agency should pay careful attention to the process of data collection in establishing goals and objectives.

Tools for Planning in a State Agency

The State Plan: The state plan, as written for Titles III and VII, provides state agencies with an opportunity to set goals, objectives, and action steps for both titles. In addition, the state plan may, and possibly should, be a vehicle for the state agency to generate goals and objectives beyond Titles III and VII. There is an advantage to incorporating goals and objectives other than those of the two titles in the plan. Since the state plan is a process whereby sanctioning occurs, the state agency will have a sanctioned goal or objective. The state plan requires the signature of the governor and approval by the organization in which the state unit of aging is located (if it is in one). If the state agency has specific requirements that it wishes to impose upon its grantees, the state plan is a viable mechanism for this purpose. If a state plan is used as a mechanism for requiring area agencies on aging and nutrition programs to comply with certain requirements of the state, then the state agency must insure that adequate input from the AAAs and Title VII programs is developed and maintained during the formulation stage of the state plan. For example, the state agency that wishes to establish and include in the state plan a statewide information and referral committee must have the cooperation of the AAAs to effectively do so.

AAA Area Plans: A state plan may include various requirements for approval of an area plan. In order for an area plan to be funded, it *must* be approved by its state agency. The area plan can be a tool in which the state agency requires the AAA to spell out any particular process or action. For example, if the state plan requires development of county councils on aging or information and referral services, the area plan may be used to describe how the AAA intends to meet this goal. The state agencies might require an AAA to document needs in the area plan in order to fund a particular project. The area plan should describe the planning process of the AAA, including details on the gathering of documentation and on the establishment of priorities.

Title VII Nutrition Project Application: The state agency may wish the nutrition projects to establish certain goals and objectives; this may be accomplished through the nutrition grant application. It certainly would be appropriate, on a year-to-year basis, to require Title VII projects to submit a plan of action for the forthcoming year.

Information and Referral Services: The information and referral services may be a coordinated network. In any case, information and referral is an appropriate means for determining what requests are being made for specific services. The state agency may wish to collect data on the following: services being requested; needs being met; and needs not being met, although requested. Information and referral services can provide a concrete idea of which needs are not being met. It may be appropriate to develop funding around unmet needs for services being requested.

Utilizing Existing Local, State, and Federal Resources: The state agency should develop a mechanism to assist in supplying information on research programs and data collection schemes. The state agency could collect copies of all research and data, so that all this information would be centrally located and available to the public. The state agency may be able to collect all information in the state in the field of housing, transportation, and medical resources from other state governmental bodies. With a significant amount of information pulled together, the process of writing grants is simplified.

Comprehensive Planning

Very few, if any, state agencies on aging are attempting to provide a comprehensive planning system.

The necessity for comprehensive planning becomes more obvious as the system itself becomes more complex. Comprehensive planning can begin at one of two points: from the top—the state agency itself—and from the bottom—individual elderly and community people at the local level. Whether the scheme begins at the top or at the bottom makes little difference, for viable comprehensive planning requires that both meet at some point.

Ideally, comprehensive planning should include all agencies or groups involved in services or actions that affect the elderly either directly or indirectly. For example, when focusing on health issues, consideration must be given to nursing homes, homemaker services, home health aides, hospitals, health maintenance organizations, comprehensive health planning, Medicaid, Medicare, dentists, doctors, companies that design prosthetic devices, and so on.

From this long list, it should be clear that comprehensive planning in all fields affecting the elderly is not feasible. The ideal must be pared down more in line with the agency's capability to coordinate and foster the necessary communications between involved agencies.

When a state agency begins its comprehensive planning efforts, it is of utmost importance that it make an assessment of current state planning. In many states, an official planning body works out of the governor's office. The state agency should attempt to integrate its planning with that of other state agencies, for sanctioning of the state's planning process is most desirable.

Another consideration that planners must take into account is that a comprehensive, well-written, thick document that incorporates all areas of service delivery for the elderly will generally not be read. Moreover, such a document is consistently too complex to implement and would produce too great a fiscal burden on the state. The point here is not that plans should not be written, but that plans should be written concisely. The major problem with the comprehensive document is in informing people of its content.

A comprehensive plan is designed to teach people what is necessary and to suggest approaches to making changes in the status quo. A comprehensive plan of this nature may serve as good documentation for legitimizing action. The best measurement of a comprehensive plan is by quantum units of change. That is, the more improvement in the quality of life of older people, the more successful the comprehensive plan. In some programs, success lies in not losing any ground. Some comprehensive plans could document the need to continue a program and to maintain its level of funding.

What is a comprehensive plan then? It is a plan that takes into account all aspects of the lives of the elderly in order to propose a mechanism, on a priority basis, that will improve their quality of life.

Comprehensive planning is accomplished through coordinating the efforts of all organizations and individuals that affect the lives of older persons. Specifically, improvement of communications within and between each of these units facilitates comprehensive planning. For example, transportation services would be interfaced and planned with health, housing, recreational, and other services. What induces the people involved in these services to participate?

The Carrot

In most meetings called to improve communication and coordination between agencies, most participants are involved for two or three sessions and then stop attending because of more pressing priorities. Each agency and representative who attends should expect to gain something from their participation. A letter of appreciation for their services is not enough. So what is the inducement to large-scale participation? Money is the carrot in this case.

Multiple funded projects have some difficulty in the administration of funds, but multiple agency applications for grants are often eagerly funded. As resources have become more scarce and money tighter, the federal government has begun to fund multiple agency proposals. For example, in one state, ACTION, the state agency, the AoA, and the state regional governmental bodies joined together to fund an information and referral system and staff support for AAAs in the amount of $500,000. A well-written grant requires the same process as good planning. It documents the needs and proposes solutions to the problems of unmet needs, and it strengthens those services currently requiring expanded support. By utilizing the *carrot* concept, the comprehensive planning mechanisms can be built around such a venture.

A Model

In assessing various agencies and departments, especially the larger ones, it becomes apparent that the midlevel positions, especially planners, have a great deal of knowledge of the workings of the organizations and interlocking networks that presently exist. A comprehensive planning mechanism might include an overall committee composed of important representatives of the service delivery system to the elderly such as homemaker programs, senior centers, nursing homes, transportation, health, housing, legal, and information and referral services. The overall committee might have a very limited role, primarily reviewing the reports from various subunits or taskforces. Each taskforce (which should be small for maximum effectiveness) could focus on a specific area of the service delivery system. These small taskforces could be composed of the various agencies and organizations in the area of concentration, e.g., transportation. If possible, each committee member should serve on at least two taskforces, thereby improving cross-communication. Their first tasks would be simply to compile the data on the agency shelves. No attempt should be made to transform the data into a comprehensive report. The data keep changing, and unless there is a specific use for them, they end up where they began: on the shelf. A simple listing of the data will suffice. The data to be collected could consist mainly of grant application information. The taskforce itself could compile this information, storing it while the summary listing is distributed statewide in order that the information will be available for grant applications.

Each service delivery area and taskforce can apply for funds from the federal government. If the taskforce efforts result in funding, then some progress will have been made toward comprehensive planning and comprehensive service delivery.

Midlevel personnel should be used on taskforces because they usually have significant knowledge of their agencies. In addition, they can probably devote more time to coordination efforts than the directors. One difficulty in using midlevel staff personnel, however, is that they are generally not empowered to make immediate decisions regarding interagency cooperation or the development of cooperative ventures. As a result, the decisions in question usually revert back to the agency director. Thus, it may be useful to restrict the taskforces to such things as pinpointing grant possibilities, collecting data and needs around these grants, and making the information known to the general community.

Options

Community agencies with the capacity to respond quickly to requests for proposals could develop a grant proposal if they had access to the necessary information. The overall coordinating committee for this comprehensive planning model should receive information on the status of each prospective grant. This committee could then develop a report synthesizing the brief reports from each taskforce into what might be considered a comprehensive plan. This, in reality, would be a comprehensive system of funding with an integrated aspect.

If such an interagency coordinating committee for the elderly were under a governor's planning committee, two options would emerge. First, it could generate a report to the governor's planning committee in an attempt to have the report submitted as part of a more formal comprehensive plan under the governor's office (if such exists). Second, a specific issue could be brought formally to the governor's office from the overall committee through the governor's planning committee.

In summary, the focus of the state agency must be statewide comprehensive planning. Such planning should duplicate neither the planning or administrative functions carried out by other state departments nor those previously delegated to AAAs. Available to the state agency are a number of related planning tools such as the state plan, AAA area plans, and Title VII nutrition project applications which provide both descriptive data and recommended goals and objectives. Finally, planning by and for the elderly should include other agencies involved in services or actions that affect older people. Support should be developed at the highest functioning level possible within state government.

4

TITLE III PROGRAMS: THE AREA AGENCY CONCEPT

James R. Jones

In discussing the development of an area agency on aging (AAA), it is important to consider that a new organization ordinarily goes through two major growth periods: its planning process and its contact or implementation process. The activities and administration of an organization and the way it defines itself to the community are quite different during the two processes. This article will trace the development of the AAA in Mobile, Alabama, and will discuss the successful negotiation of the planning and implementation stages of its growth. Before looking at these activities, a brief general discussion of the area agency concept will be presented.

A New Concept: Area Agencies on Aging

The Older Americans Act of 1965, and as amended, has attempted to focus community, state, and national attention on the specific needs of the elderly. In 1969, Title III of the act addressed itself to state and community planning for services delivered to the elderly. This planning orientation represented a departure from the original Title III concept, which was to fund direct service programs in local communities to provide social services to the elderly. Although over 1,000 individual projects around the country had been funded in this way, the desired impact on the elderly community was never achieved. Recommendations of the 1971 White House Conference on Aging pointed directly to the need for more coordination and planning on the local level for services to the elderly. Although major funding was not available, new policy initiatives on the national level began to change toward a planning orientation to help shape a new Title III concept.

A special revenue-sharing approach initiated by the Nixon administration in 1972 resulted in new legislation for social services, health, manpower, and community development. Thereafter, programs for the elderly formerly funded by categorical grants would have to compete at state and local levels for revenue-sharing funds in these program areas. This new competitive situation seemed to call for an aging structure at the substate level to coordinate local resources as well as for a unit on aging at the state level. Further, concomitant with new aging program strategies, a reorganization was taking place in many states which consolidated a wide variety of programs into large departments of human resources. The various programs in these new umbrella agencies, which could also serve older persons, had a much higher level of funding than the Administration on Aging (AoA) would have in the foreseeable future. This situation seemed to require state and local agencies to focus on influencing the funding plans of other programs. This allied services approach called for cross-program planning by those new departments of human resources and allowed for the transfer of funds between programs. As these new state departments of human resources emerged, typically staffed by central planning personnel, the need for planning and coordination and for advocates to direct the resources of these agencies on behalf of the elderly became more and more evident.

1973 Amendments

The results of these activities precipitated the 1973 amendments to the Older Americans Act which made the AoA the federal focal point and advocate for older persons and established a network of state units on aging as well as AAAs. These state and substate units were charged with gradually bringing about comprehensive coordinated service systems to meet the needs of older persons throughout the nation. Presently, the Title III program outreaches to a wide variety of other public and private service programs and mandates a planner-catalyst-advocate role at federal, state, and substate levels, an omnibus role which has no successful model to follow.

Definition of the AAA Concept

Since the area agency concept was new in 1973, organizations designated as AAAs had the initial task of defining themselves to their local communities in ways that would not only be acceptable but would also elicit the cooperation and support of those organizations that already delivered services to the elderly. To this end, the area agency in Mobile utilized the following format to define and publicize itself to the local community.

Area Agency on Aging Organizational Goals: The AAA in Mobile, Alabama, is a department of the South Alabama Regional Planning Commission (SARPC). It was designated an AAA by the State Commission on Aging as the official organization to plan, evaluate, coordinate, and, where feasible, contract for the delivery of existing or expanded services to the elderly throughout the south Alabama region. The organizational goals of the AAA are as follows:

1. Investigation—To investigate the needs of the elderly and the resources presently available to meet those needs.
2. Planning—To plan the expansion of present services and/or create new service programs for the elderly.
3. Dissemination—To disseminate information in the form of training, educational programs, seminars, and the like concerning present and potential service programs for the elderly.
4. Coordination—To coordinate with existing service organizations, senior citizens' groups, and governmental agencies for the development of a cooperative delivery system.
5. Pooling—To pool available or untapped resources to be utilized on behalf of the elderly.
6. Promotion—To promote the cause of the elderly and seek to enhance their independence within our society.
7. Contract—To contract for the delivery of expanded social services to the elderly with existing service organizations throughout the community.
8. Evaluation—To evaluate the effectiveness of the service delivery system and seek to insure that services proposed and those being implemented are providing significant opportunities for independent living to the recipients.

With these organizational goals in mind, we will now review the planning phase of the organization's activities and examine some of the reasoning behind the choices made in implementing the program.

The Planning Phase

On October 1, 1972, SARPC, in cooperation with the Alabama State Commission on Aging, began to prepare a broadly conceived, cooperatively developed, and mutually agreed upon, comprehensive areawide plan for delivery of services to the elderly in the region. This planning process was made possible under special funds granted by the AoA to states that wanted to develop comprehensive plans as a preliminary effort before AoA implemented the area agency concept on a nationwide basis. Alabama, one of ten states to take advantage of this opportunity to do preliminary planning, designated six areawide aging projects; the Areawide Model Project in Mobile was one of these six.

The project area comprised three counties in a land mass of 4,177 square miles. One of the counties was urban and highly industrialized; the other two were rural agricultural counties. The total population numbered 411,596 persons, 51,368 of whom were sixty years of age and older. Minorities comprised 27.2 percent of the elderly population in the region. It was estimated that there were approximately 18,451 older citizens whose incomes were below the poverty threshold (35 percent of all the elderly in the region).

When planning for the Mobile Areawide Model Project began, there was one "old" Title III (direct services delivery) program operating in the region. The program was located in a senior citizens' highrise facility sponsored by the Housing Board. Two Community Action Program (CAP) agencies in the region were providing outreach and transportation to the elderly as part of their overall program. Operation Mainstream was providing twenty part-time jobs to elderly citizens, and there were state-supported welfare programs. Although a commodities program existed in the rural counties and food stamps were available in the urban counties, there was little coordination and communication between the various service agencies. To facilitate coordination between agencies and to gather much needed information, the Areawide Model Project organized a regional taskforce.

Taskforce and Advisory Council

The first meeting of the regional taskforce was held on November 7, 1972, with thirty-eight members attending, representing local governments, social service agencies, and senior citizens' organizations. The Areawide Model Project suggested that such a county taskforce be formed because of the great geographical area that the planning agency covered in its activities. Subsequently, three county taskforces were organized with a total of 134 members for the region, 24 of whom were governmental representatives, 50 service providers, and 60 representatives from senior citizens' organizations.

Each county taskforce defined its functions as follows:

1. To assist in identifying the needs of the elderly and to evaluate the priorities of those needs.
2. To assist in creating a comprehensive regional plan for meeting these needs.
3. To assist in identifying the community resources useful in implementing the program.
4. To assist in creating community awareness of the problems of the elderly and in nurturing a spirit of cooperation in working towards a solution to these problems.

At each county taskforce meeting, committees were immediately organized to address the functions of conducting a needs survey and a resources survey, planning a nutritional program, and providing publicity for the new organization. These committees were chaired by representatives of the planning agency until an articulate leader within each respective committee could be identified.

One of the mistakes often made in community organizations is to give volunteers too much responsibility too soon, as a result of which volunteers soon become overwhelmed and no longer attend meetings. By nurturing the committees and the county taskforces until natural leaders emerged, the Areawide Model Project staff was able to develop an effective community organization network. Since the committees had an opportunity to function and to make reports at county taskforce meetings, eventually enough was known about the members that county chairmen, along with officers, were elected. The county taskforces were able to become autonomous groups to fill the role of advocate for the elderly in each respective county.

This method of using separate county taskforces and the planning agency as the activities coordinator for the three county taskforces was utilized until the Aerawide Model Project moved into its implementation stage. At this time, each county elected representatives to a regional steering committee, which later became the Advisory Committee under the requirements of the 1973 amendments to the Older Americans Act.

Directory of Senior Citizens

In order to identify the needs of the elderly citizens, it was soon determined that the elderly first had to be located. The Areawide Model Project assumed the task of compiling a regional directory of all persons sixty years of age and older who had specific needs. In order to reach the elderly citizen with the greatest needs, this directory was restricted to those individuals who were isolated either socially or geographically, who lived alone, who were in need of social services that were not being provided, or who had health problems that might require institutionalization if health services were not delivered in the community. The 1970 Census information and the Alabama Social Indicators study conducted by the Center for the Study of Aging for the Alabama Commission on Aging in 1971 had indicated that there would be nearly 5,000 elderly citizens with these problems living in the three-county south Alabama region.

Social service organizations that were serving the elderly were asked to provide means of individuals who met these criteria. Since state law protects the confidentiality of those individuals who receive services from state-supported programs, these individuals had to be called and their permission obtained to add their names to the directory list. With the assistance of the social service agencies, local civic groups, senior citizens' organizations, and church groups, the directory was finally compiled. In the first printing of the directory, over 8,000 elderly citizens were identified. Since the regions had been divided into sixteen social service planning subunits utilizing census tract identification, the directory names were divided into these sixteen regions. This directory became the basis for outreach activities and furnished a mailing list for providing information concerning new services available to the elderly throughout the region.

The Organization of Senior Citizens' Groups

Early in the program, it was determined that two of the greatest needs of senior citizens were for social contact and for an organized voice within their local communities. To assist this effort, the Areawide Model Project agreed to conduct three training programs to help organize task-oriented senior citizens' groups. The purpose of these training programs was to give the participants information on how a senior citizens' group can become an active force in the community for dealing with the needs of the elderly.

Specific instructions were given on how to recruit and organize a senior citizens' group, how to design social activities and group tasks, how to develop interesting programs, how to build group identification, how to develop good community relations, and how to run meetings and conduct successful projects. The average training program lasted five hours and was spread out over a morning and afternoon. Most of the participants represented senior citizens' groups or individuals who desired to organize a senior citizens' group within their own area. To supplement this effort, a Community Organization Training Manual was developed.

Twelve new organizations were formed in the three-county region. Many of the old senior citizens' groups, which had been social clubs and had been meeting once a month, became task-oriented and more involved in the community. Utilizing the above format, the Areawide Model Project staff successfully assisted in the organization of thirty-three task-oriented senior citizens' groups during the first two years of its planning and implementation efforts.

Needs Survey

Each county taskforce organized a needs survey committee to determine the needs of the elderly citizens in each respective county. The results of these efforts were utilized in a needs survey instrument. Each committee was composed of over 50 percent elderly citizens. A statistical sample was taken from the senior citizens' directory to be interviewed using the needs survey instrument.

Some 300 volunteers from the south Alabama region, representing senior citizens' organizations, home demonstration clubs, colleges and junior colleges, Jaycettes, nursing home auxiliaries, and service organizations, were trained to conduct the interviews. Although the use of volunteers made the project more difficult than utilizing paid professional interviewers would have been, the project director felt that the large number of volunteers becoming involved with the needs of the elderly would help redirect the community's attention to the concerns of the elderly. This notion proved to be true.

Prior to the initiation of the survey, interviewer training sessions were held in each county. In these sessions, interviewers were instructed in interviewing techniques, were familiarized with the contents of the questionnaires, and were assigned interview names. To facilitate control of field work and subsequent data analysis, the three-county area was divided into sixteen subareas.

Interviews were conducted from February 15, 1973, to March 1, 1973. Each interviewer carried a letter of endorsement signed by a county commissioner and the sheriff. If a respondent was not at home when the interviewer called, at least two callbacks were made in an attempt to complete the interview. Respondent substitutions were not allowed except in cases where the respondent was deceased. When replacements were made, names were randomly selected from a list of persons from the deceased respondent's immediate locality.

Upon completion of the interviews, questionnaires were checked for errors and prepared for electronic data processing. Subsequently, two series of computer runs were made to analyze the survey data. The first series consisted of tabulations of aggregate responses and was used to ascertain general response characteristics. The second series developed high-, medium-, and low-risk profiles of elderly persons most likely to require social services in the community. The following criteria were used to determine a respondent's risk profile: (1) under sixty-five years of age, (2) annual household income of $3,000 or more, (3) ownership of an automobile or easy access to transportation, (4) telephone available in the home, (5) residence with one or more persons, (6) close contact with another person most of the time, (7) excellent, good, or fair health, (8) ability to carry out doctor's instructions without assistance, and (9) ability to go up and down stairs and do housework. Respondents who met eight of the above criteria were classified as low risk; those who met six or seven, medium risk; and those who met five or less, high risk.

The results of the survey indicated the priority of needs of the elderly to be: (1) additional income supplements, (2) health needs and related services, (3) opportunity for social interaction, (4) information concerning social services (information and referral), (5) nutrition, and (6) better housing.

Resource Survey

The county taskforces appointed resource committees which were responsible for identifying resources in their respective counties, as well as for assisting in creating a comprehensive plan to expand these services. To perform this duty, the committees sought to identify the agencies already providing services in the county; the agencies needed in the county but not in operation; the community assistance (funding) needed to meet the demand of the agencies that would provide needed services; and those resources that were available and that could be rechanneled to fulfill the needs of the elderly.

In order to meet these survey requirements, the resource committee designed a survey instrument. Over 100 service organizations were interviewed by the resource committee to determine the extent of the services being provided to the elderly by existing agencies. The results of this survey provided the necessary information to establish a plan for developing multipurpose centers for the elderly throughout the region.

Following the guidelines of the original planning grant, the project staff began to develop proposals for implementing new and expanded services to the elderly throughout the region. The comprehensive plan included nutritional, information and referral service, multipurpose center service, and proposed homemaker/home health care service components. After reviewing the available resources, it was determined that the first three service components could be implemented under the auspices of the Areawide Model Project and that the homemaker/home health care service could come under the auspices of the State Welfare Department, since its state charter provided for that type of service once it was approved by the State Welfare Department.

During this time, the 1973 amendments to the Older Americans Act were passed by Congress, and the Areawide Model Project (located within SARPC) was designated as the AAA for south Alabama. This action gave the Planning Commission legal authority to apply for funds and to contract for services in the community at the local level. This propelled the new AAA from the planning stage into the implementation stage.

The Implementation Process

Moving from the planning to the implementation stage of community service produces many problems. During planning, organizations will generally share their ideas and assist in cooperative efforts. Once money becomes available to fund projects, however, hard decisions must be made on who will implement the projects, and competition often arises. These realities soon were brought to bear in the south Alabama region as the area agency sought to implement its comprehensive plan.

Senior Activities for Independent Living

The AAA, seeing the need for coordinated delivery of social services as a priority problem among the elderly, applied for Title VII funds to assist in developing multipurpose centers throughout the region. Title VII, a nutritional program for the elderly, besides providing nourishing meals for the elderly, would serve as a catalyst for assembling a number of services to be delivered at congregate meal sites. Using information from the needs and resource surveys, the AAA divided the region into sixteen social service areas and set up a nutritional committee. It was determined that the best utilization of resources would be via development of a multipurpose center within each of these service areas.

Since preliminary information indicated there would not be enough resources to support a center in each of the service areas, decisions had to be made on which service areas would receive the service centers. The agency called upon its regional taskforce and nutritional committee to help devise a way to rank the various service areas. It was hoped that through this process all communities would accept whatever decisions the ranking process produced. The criteria for ranking each service area were as follows: the number of (1) elderly who lived in the area, (2) minorities, (3) elderly with transportation problems, (4) elderly who lived alone, (5) elderly seventy-five years of age and older, and (6) elderly with an income below the poverty level. It was felt that these criteria addressed the needs of both the rural and urban areas. Subsequently, it was suggested that ten multipurpose centers be instituted, five of them located in rural areas and five in urban areas.

In order to convey to the community the philosophical concept behind these multipurpose centers and services to the elderly, this program was called Senior Activities for Independent Living (SAIL). Title VII and Title III resources were coordinated with those services available in each local community, and ten multipurpose centers for the elderly were established in the region. Not only were the eight coordinated social services required by Title VII provided, but a multiplicity of activities were carried on as desired and sponsored by the center participants. One of the primary goals was to set up each center as an autonomous unit for services to the elderly, with the ultimate responsibility for finding complete community support for its operations within the next three years.

Five of the SAIL centers were operated by minorities. Total participation numbered between 1,800 and 2,200 persons each week, with over 60 percent of the participation being minority or low-income. During the first year of operation, 212 volunteers logged over 24,000 hours assisting the implementation of the program.

Information and Referral

One of the primary needs of the elderly in the area was to obtain information on existing and expanded services available to them throughout the region. The AAA initiated a plan to develop a sophisticated information data bank concerning all services directly or indirectly related to the needs of the elderly. The AAA then organized a regionwide information and referral (I&R) committee to investigate the feasibility of utilizing a computer to handle the information on resources. The I&R committee endorsed the AAA's approach to organizing a computerized information data base and took the responsibility of directing this program for the whole region.

This referral program evolved into a comprehensive I&R program, with the area agency contributing some of its resources for the development of the information base and the I&R committee developing community resources to run the referral program. This effort refocused the attention of community agencies and organizations upon the needs of the elderly and unearthed new resources that could be developed for serving them.

One factor in the successful development of this computerized approach to I&R was the emphasis it gave to utilizing the data obtained by the planning agency. The I&R committee pointed out that planners would be able to identify gaps in the service system as well as weaknesses in the service system caused by eligibility restrictions, insufficient capacity of service agencies, and limits imposed by the large geographical area served. The data would also aid in studies to plan for an overall transportation and service network as well as the presentation of training workshops for professional persons according to job categories. The data would also help coordinate the client population.

Through the central telephone I&R service, all known data on human services in the area were made available free of charge to anyone. Therefore, an inquirer could obtain a list of agencies that provided the services needed, according to his particular eligibility factors and specific needs.

A total of 825 surveys of agencies and organizations were completed, and this material was printed into factbooks especially designed for the service agencies. Based on the directory that the area agency had begun the previous year, a smaller and less complex book especially designed for the elderly was printed and mailed directly to 14,000 senior citizens.

Organizational Development

Since there had been a tremendous change in the Title III regulations defining the tasks of the area agencies, the director began an internal evaluation process. After the 1973 amendments, the duties of the area agency were specified to be much broader and more involved than had been originally conceived. Further concern was generated when staff members indicated they were no longer sure of their exact roles within the organization or if what their functions or duties would be under the new proposed plan of action.

To address these concerns, the director instituted an organization development process utilizing a Management by Objectives: Organizational Development (MBO-OD) model. His purpose was to build a true employee team and to weld individual effort into a common cause. The philosophical concept for this approach was based on the belief that each member of the team, regardless of his position in the organization, needed to understand the objectives of the whole organization and to be able to see how his individual performance contributed to the overall objectives.

Several training sessions were designed, taught by a consultant from the Center for the Study of Aging at the University of Alabama. These sessions included defining new opportunities within the agency, restating personnel goals, redesigning job descriptions, and redefining the organizational goals of the area agency. The most significant discovery made in this process was that, contrary to the physical planning role of a traditional planning commission, the area agency was now defining itself in terms of new roles in the community. These roles involved coordination, pooling of resources, promoting the cause of the elderly, contracting for services, and evaluating social services.

Other outcomes of the MBO-OD process were expansion of the staff to include a grants management specialist, greater involvement by the Advisory Committee, and development of a GANTT chart for all functional areas of the area agency. As a result of the internal organizational changes and the new visibility of the agency, the city of Mobile decided to divert its resources designated for serving the elderly to the area agency for distribution according to the area agency's priorities.

Funding

The changes that the area agency experienced in working in the community may be demonstrated in quantifiable terms by reviewing the funding levels. The program began with an Areawide Model Project planning grant of $60,000 to develop a comprehensive delivery system for services to the elderly. Utilizing Title III and Title VII, revenue-sharing, and other community resources, the program in its first year of implementation was able to raise $400,000 for the development of the ten multipurpose centers. In addition, the Areawide Model Project was able to obtain commitments from the community to divert $246,000 of local community resources for the maintenance and development of these centers. At the end of the second year, the total cash resources of the agency now designated an AAA exceeded $550,000, with the community committing $308,000 for the expansion and development of the ten multipurpose centers. Meals-on-Wheels, day care, and a transportation linkage system were operating throughout the region.

Evaluation

Under the Title III regulations, a community must have a significant voice in the planning process. Although the area agency had tremendous community support, the sharing of responsibility for evaluation and contracting with the Advisory Committee that represented community service agencies, local municipal governments, and consumers was not an easy matter. The AAA director felt that such a diversity of membership was necessary because several members of the Advisory Committee also represented agencies with which the area agency had service contracts. The Advisory Committee was called together for the purpose of reviewing the results of the internal organization process that had occurred. Under each of the organizational goals, a functional statement was developed, as well as a description of how this goal might be implemented within the community. The Advisory Committee was also given information on proposed funding sources, and it discussed its projected responsibility for evaluating all local agencies that received funds from the area agency. As a result of this session, the Advisory Committee asked for meaningful criteria to be used in evaluating existing service agencies in the community.

The area agency contracted with the Center for the Study of Aging to conduct a third-party evaluation of each of the multipurpose centers. The agency wanted not only to determine the impact of the new services upon the elderly participants, but also to be able to compare the relative effectiveness of the individual service centers. This evaluation examined changes in health, activity levels, mobility, sociability, financial well-being, and adjustment to aging. The concluding remarks of the evaluation were: "The SAIL Program has seemingly served as a catalyst in helping the elderly accept and adjust to the aging process and perhaps more importantly has done so in such a way as to make life more meaningful for them."

Although the SAIL Program originally centered on meeting the nutritional needs of an aging population, the above observations suggest that the multi-purpose concept of the program has been fulfilled. The data indicated that many other benefits were being realized by the elderly through their attendance at the centers. The respondents surveyed especially mentioned the benefits of information services at the centers. This finding reinforced the idea that the elderly need an organized structure within which they may learn of and have access to social, medical, political, and financial opportunities. It is believed that the SAIL Program, with few exceptions, has made those opportunities available.

Process of Allocating Resources

Following the recommendations of the Advisory Committee, the area agency developed a step-by-step procedure for allocating the resources of the organization. This procedure was presented to the Advisory Committee, approved, and publicized to the general community. It required three months for its total implementation. The following is a brief description of the steps.

1. *Public Hearing*—As required by Title III, a public hearing was held to discuss the area plan. All senior citizens' organizations and elderly persons were invited to come and discuss the priority needs of the elderly in the community and the resources available to meet those needs, and to make recommendations and changes concerning the area plan.

2. *Request for Proposals*—Following the approval of the area plan, the area agency publicly announced its request for proposals from any organization eligible to contract for the provision of social services under the priorities established in the area plan, Title III, Title VII, or by local funding sources. Any organization that met the criteria of the Older Americans Act for eligibility to conduct activities and services under the area plan on behalf of the area agency was allowed to submit a proposal. The proposals were required to contain a specific plan of action for delivery of the services, a description of how the agency coordinated with other service providers within the community, the measurable objectives the contractor would seek to achieve during the following year, a complete description of present resources the agency was allocating in the service area, and a descriptive budget detailing the use of the requested funds.

3. *Committee Review*—The area agency utilized its many working committees and the nutritional project councils to review each of the proposals and make recommendations or to request additional information from the proposed contractors. These committees included 50 percent elderly persons and had broad cross-sectional community support.

4. *Advisory Committee Review*—The Advisory Committee, as the policy-making committee of the AAA, carefully reviewed all proposals submitted by the various committees. It compared these proposals with the results of the evaluation conducted by the Center for the Study of Aging on the effectiveness of each multipurpose center's operation. It then made suggested allocations of

Title VII, Title III, and local resources. Based on the Advisory Committee's recommendations, preliminary contracts were negotiated with all organizations.

5. *Approval of Contracts*—The Executive Committee of SARPC has the fiscal authority for the planning agency. Since the AAA was (and is) a department of the regional planning commission, the area agency submitted its recommended budget for discussion, review, modification, and approval of the Executive Committee. This final step insured that the local governmental organizations which the area agency attempted to serve would make the final decisions on allocating resources for services to the elderly. Once the Executive Committee approved the budget, the contracts were submitted to the Alabama Commission on Aging for review, comments, and approval.

Support

This open process of resource allocation produced tremendous community support, as evidenced by the increased funding level from the community. It also meant that the community agreed with the priorities for allocation. Since the area agency was able to fund only ten multipurpose centers in twenty-one communities, this decision-making process permitted the area agency to continue to function in the whole region without incurring any accusation that it had been discriminatory in its allocation of resources and without causing any community to work against its efforts.

Conclusion

This article has reviewed some of the processes that the AAA in the South Alabama Regional Planning and Development Area completed to carry out its mandate during its first two years of activity. The agency went through a major organizational change when it switched from planning into implementation. Since its funding levels from Title III, Title VII, and local community resources have probably reached their maximum level, the agency is preparing to go through its next major organizational change. Besides insuring the continual flow of federal, state, and local resources, contracting for services, and evaluating the effectiveness of those delivery services, what will the new role of the area agency be like?

The role of advocate on behalf of the elderly will become stronger. Area agency personnel will be expected to work with local groups for legislative action, for the removal of architectural barriers, and for heightening the community's consciousness of the valuable input that its elderly citizens may contribute to the community's life. Such activity is already visible in this agency's promotion of an ombudsman program to protect the rights of elderly persons in nursing homes, as well as in its support and assistance in researching protective services legislation for the elderly.

Technical assistance to other social service organizations will become a major activity for the area agency. As planners and proposal writers who know useful evaluative tools for looking at the effectiveness of social services, the area agency staff will greatly enhance the staffs of other organizations within the community. Some of the activities already engaged in included assistance to a local organization in applying for and obtaining funds for a Meals-on-Wheels program in its local community and assistance to the State Welfare Department in writing a proposal for a model project for day care for older adults. Further, through membership on the boards of other social service organizations, as they complete their comprehensive plans each year, area agency representatives insure that those plans include expanded services for the elderly.

Area agency activities have given communities a new awareness of their elderly citizens. They have brought a new challenge to the elderly themselves to remain involved and active in their own communities. Most importantly, the area agency belongs to the community, and it has been successful because the community has chosen to be responsible to itself.

PART II
Direct Services

5

DIRECT SERVICES TO THE AGED

Gerald L. Euster

It is widely acknowledged that the elderly have received a less than adequate share of professional care and social services in our health and welfare system. In nations where there is considerable care for the elderly, action rarely has occurred without public pressure. Marvin R. Koller writes that "fortuitous social structures either granted great power to the aged or left them vulnerable to suffering and neglect." Koller reflects the stark reality that, for most of recorded history, the needs of the elderly have been met, at best, begrudgingly. [1]

In the United States, this fact often is dramatized harshly through the media in their exposés dealing with institutionalized, rural, and dislocated elderly citizens. Evidence that the elderly are overlooked and devalued emerges each October when millions of Americans dig deep into their pockets to contribute to hundreds of United Way fund-raising drives. Rarely, if ever, are citizens aware of—or do they question—the relatively small amounts of funds that are directed to a relatively small number of agencies and programs for the elderly.

Dr. Robert N. Butler, well known for his contributions to psychiatry and gerontology, estimated that in 1970 there were about three million older people with significant psychiatric problems who were not receiving help. He cited a report of the Biometry Branch of the National Institute of Mental Health, which concluded that if present mental health service trends continue through 1980, about 80 percent of the elderly who need assistance will not be served. Butler indicated that only 2 to 5 percent of older persons are on the rolls of community mental health centers and public and nonprofit clinics. [2]

The plight of the institutionalized elderly has been examined in great depth in the past several years. Michael Harrington has provided a vivid picture of those members of our aging population who have become a significant part of *The Other America*. [3] He believes that the practice in the United States is to "maintain" many of our aged—to give them the gift of life and at the same time to destroy for them the possibility of retaining dignity. According to Harrington, society accepts the "storage bin" philosophy toward the maintenance of the aged. The disengagement of elderly people from society is to a certain extent externally imposed.

More recent studies have reported on the collective callousness among some nursing home owners and operators who profit from the dehumanizing and substandard levels of care afforded older people. The Nader study group report, for example, has aroused interest among the public and its lawmakers to work to raise standards of humane care in institutional settings. The report further suggests that those few homes that are humane, competent, and mindful of their residents' need for activity and meaning in their day "highlight the staggering gap between what an affluent society should attain and what is too frequently the reality for most nursing homes."[4]

Improvement of the quality of life for residents of nursing homes and homes for the aged will continue to remain a problem until the residential care industry is forced to redesign its product in line with well-conceived alternative programs and provisions for the aged. There will always be a need for institutional arrangements for the elderly, but the future is certain to awaken in the public and consumers the potential value of multiservice centers, combining homemaker, nutritional, day care, transportation-escort, and social recreational programs. These alternatives will insure that institutional care, if used judiciously, will become a rehabilitative tool rather than a final sentence for its residents.

It would be grossly unfair to label all institutional programs faulty and irresponsibly conceived. The Philadelphia Geriatric Center, the Dallas Home for the Jewish Aged, the Drexel Home for the Aged in Chicago, the Carmelite Homes in Connecticut, and the Mansfield Homes in Ohio are among the leaders in a field that is beginning to respond to public scrutiny and demands for accountability. The recent research of the Philadelphia Geriatric Center demonstrating the treatability of the mentally impaired aged attests to the leadership and innovation that is beginning to emerge in the nursing home industry.[5]

That the elderly are becoming recognized as worthy of special consideration in many communities is reinforced by the multitude of preretirement seminars and courses sponsored by industries and agencies, telephone reassurance programs for the homebound, and various plans for supplying well-balanced meals to large groups of the elderly. Additional recognition of this age group is provided in communities that reduce public transportation fares, provide homestead tax exemptions, and offer special admission prices to civic attractions. Public housing projects for those persons who meet eligibility requirements offer a useful form of low-rent congregate living, often accompanied by a wide range of social and recreational services. Many colleges and universities are beginning to develop attractive course offerings in an attempt to recruit older Americans.

Innovative programs are being designed throughout the country. The state of South Carolina and Clemson University cooperate to offer an exciting camping program for the elderly. In San Antonio, the public library permits elderly borrowers to telephone in a request for a title, and if the book is available, it is mailed out at library expense. Large communities frequently sponsor information and referral centers to assist the elderly to understand what services are available and to help them make an initial connection.

In the following pages, the planning process and direct services in the community will be examined in greater detail. Services and technologies for the institutionalized elderly will be discussed to demonstrate what can be accomplished to upgrade the quality of life for those citizens who find themselves away from their natural environment. It is hoped that the section on services to the institutionalized will allay the fears of those who believe that all homes for the aged and nursing care facilities tend to victimize the elderly psychologically.

Planning for the Elderly

Particularly since the 1961 and 1971 White House Conferences on Aging, "planning" has become a keyword in the expression of American concern for elderly citizens. During the past fifteen years, millions of elderly people have gained from protection under Medicare, expanding Social Security benefits, and community services that have evolved from the Older Americans Act and from the law that prohibits age discrimination in employment. Federal, state, and local planning, along with significant legislation, have led to the most substantial gains ever achieved by older persons in our nation. We have witnessed remarkable changes in the quality of health care, rehabilitation, housing, employment, recreation, and continuing education services, among many others, and we appear to be well on the way toward facing up to what former Secretary of Health, Education, and Welfare Wilbur Cohen has called "The Challenge of the Aging."[6]

Public Planning

It is widely believed that a prerequisite to any further achievement of our specific goals and objectives for elderly Americans is a more systematic organization and delivery of services carried out through a process of public planning. The term *public* planning is used in this discussion to stress the mandate of the 1971 White House Conference on Aging, in which the delegates made specific recommendations that planning not only be based upon the experience and expertise of professional personnel and specialists in aging, but that it also include early, and on a continuous basis, a greater representation of the elderly. Racial and ethnic minority groups representing the elderly, together with middle-aged and young persons, were to be included in the planning process.[7] The continuing interest of the Administration on Aging (AoA) in the planning process was expressed in 1975:

Important to realistic and successful planning for programs and services which address the actual needs of older persons is the participation of the recipients themselves in some aspects of the planning process. Representation of older persons from diverse groups is meant to assure that the real priority needs of all target groups are addressed in the planning of services. While State and Area agencies are expected to foster consumer participation, they need to know the different ways of including the older person in their planning process which will contribute most effectively to the development and implementation of plans for the coordination of resources for the elderly. [8]

An encouraging theme running through the various White House conference recommendations for action was the developmental view of the elderly citizen in his later years. Indeed, the participants viewed the later years of life as a time of new opportunity, fulfillment, and growth, and not as a period of conflict, sadness, and decline in functioning.

Among the various recommendations for planning were the following:

1. It was strongly believed that the planning activities of the three levels of government in the area of aging should be interrelated, and that planning of the state and local levels should receive financial support from the federal government.
2. During all planning stages, the development of the plan should be coordinated with the state agency on aging. Mechanisms should be set up to provide systematic federal and state evaluations of planning in aging.
3. Multigenerational programs and services should be targeted so as to insure that their efforts are more responsive to the concerns and needs of the elderly.
4. If federal revenue sharing is enacted, the legislation should provide for the protection of the elderly's interests.
5. Special consideration should be given to the needs of older persons who belong to minority groups, since racial and ethnic discrimination, with its attendant consequences, has subjected many members of these groups to low levels of income, health, and housing provisions.

Since the 1971 White House Conference on Aging, state agencies working in behalf of the elderly have increased in size and importance. The AoA guidelines for state agencies were specified in 1970 as follows:

The State Plan will project staffing for a three year period and must include qualified staff to undertake these responsibilities: research, data gathering, and information dissemination; program review and evaluation; coordination with other agencies; staff training, consultation to other agencies; public information; citizen participation, volunteer, and advisory committee activities; and administrative and management work.

The AoA guidelines also indicated that states should coordinate and stimulate planning efforts on behalf of all older persons, and that effective working relationships should be developed and maintained with other public and private agencies dealing with the elderly. In order to increase the effectiveness of services, ongoing evaluations of aging problems, consultation, and technical and information services were to be provided to organizations working with the aged. [9]

Leadership Planning

Dr. Robert Binstock, in preparing the background and issues document on "Planning" for the 1971 White House Conference on Aging, defined the central challenge for establishing effective leadership planning in aging: namely, to develop more powerful resources for influencing existing organizations to change their policies and patterns of operation so as to better serve the elderly. [10] Binstock believes that we have created mechanisms for leadership planning and that this aspect of the goals of planning in aging has been realized. However, "the various planning mechanisms have been relatively ineffective in getting generic organizations to be more responsible to the needs of the aging, because they have relied upon relatively weak resources for exercising power—data on unmet needs, moral legitimacy, presumed prestige or status, and energy and commitment." Binstock asserts that the key source of power for influencing public or voluntary organizations is broad popular support. Such support is necessary for acquiring regulatory control and for obtaining the funds necessary to carry out the work. According to Binstock, popular support has always been a prime influence on legislators and elected administrative officials. For more effective planning in aging to emerge in this decade, these resources for power will probably need to be developed. [11]

To be sure, the past several years have witnessed a vast public awareness of the needs of the aged. Considerable research has been originated within universities and state and voluntary agencies in an attempt to establish new knowledge and effective technologies for serving the elderly. Each year, the AoA prepares a substantial research and development strategy document to help potential researchers in the field to better understand research priorities as determined by the federal government. The AoA and other federal agencies concerned with the aged are extremely cognizant of the role of research knowledge as a further basis for rational public policy and planning.

Needs of the Future

As a nation, we are overcoming traditional beliefs and myths about the elderly and are making more rational attempts to provide them with more viable public and voluntary services. To a greater extent, the elderly themselves are becoming a political force that is certain to mold public policy in future years. Organizations such as the Gray Panthers, the American Association of Retired Persons, and the National Council on Aging, along with hundreds of other organizations in the field, suggest a vast resource for exerting constructive power within the legislative and community arenas. Once the elderly are recognized as an important political and social force, services and programs will emerge not "begrudgingly" but as a rational response to our temporary lapse in humanity. The end result—and it cannot be in the too distant future— will be a national policy for the elderly that will guarantee their fuller participation in community life. At the very least, elderly citizens will be given choices pertaining to their continuing involvement.

For many years to come, programs and services for the elderly will emerge and thrive, as state commissions and departments are held accountable for executing statewide programs to meet the needs of this group. Such state organizations will continue to encourage and assist the development of innovative programs in cities, towns, and counties and other planning areas. State organizations will provide qualitative guidance to local planning groups in direct relation to their knowledge of gerontology, their ability to utilize research, their understanding of community organization, and their expertise in consultation to social agencies and programs.

A crucial need in the next few years is to recruit as the administrators of state agencies specialists in gerontology who are trained in social work, service delivery, social planning, research, and the various disciplines identified with the elderly. Hopefully, political appointees and persons with no formal training in gerontology will be replaced through attrition. The elderly themselves will be used at the planning level.

To improve social services for the elderly, human service personnel at the state and local levels must tap the accumulated practice and knowledge of private-voluntary agency personnel, and with these persons design and coordinate services that will promote a satisfactory aging process. Services should be addressed to physical and social health. In the area of social health, programs and services must be created to foster the social roles, status, and self-esteem of the elderly.

Service Populations

Among the elderly there are various population groups to whom services must be addressed. On one level are the elderly who can benefit from the services of social clubs, multipurpose centers, retirement communities, congregate dining, and various forms of day programs. Such persons tend to be physically and psychologically capable of taking on new experiences in social relations and, through carefully selected activities, of using their leisure time constructively. Some in this group tend to use these agencies and services to reconstruct, realistically or symbolically, former family and societal roles.

Many older persons, following the retirement or death of spouse and friends, make excellent use of such programs. Jewish community centers, neighborhood centers, and, in more recent years, Foster Grandparent Programs and volunteer service centers have brought many of the elderly back into the mainstream of community life. For this group, social services are truly "developmental" and contribute to satisfactory aging.

On another level are older Americans who are prevented from benefitting from these programs because of access factors. Lack of transportation, a physical handicap, the illness of a spouse, or personal illness may weaken the motivation of such persons. Children, especially when they live a great distance from their elderly parents, cannot be depended upon to escort them to community activities. At-home visits, occasional church activities, and special events in the lives of grandchildren—graduations, recitals, bar mitzvahs, and parties—tend to become the staple activities that provide satisfactions for this group.

A third group of elderly Americans consists of those who remain generally unserved by social agencies, uninvolved with family or friends, and disengaged from the pursuit of meaningful life activities. While we have no accurate count of such persons, it would be safe to assume that this target group tends to live in virtual seclusion from others, possibly suffering from loneliness and a sense of defeat. Many such persons are likely living in the community following several years of hospitalization in chronic patient wards of state hospitals. A large number of these people, formerly "dumped" into hospitals, have now been "dumped" back into the community. Nursing homes, long-term care facilities, foster home placements, and, in some places, welfare hotels have become an alternative form of isolation for many of them. Jean M. Maxwell succinctly describes the potential impact of disengagement:

> One of the major impacts of retirement and/or aging is the potential increase of time spent by oneself. Being alone can be enjoyable, fruitful, and revitalizing when it is a voluntary choice made by the individual, when aloneness is rooted in the security of being loved and wanted, and when the individual is equipped with individual pursuits that interest or challenge him. Spending time by oneself can be a devastating, personally destroying experience when it is imposed—when there is no other choice. Loneliness can cripple and destroy.[12]

Institutional Living

Considerable research and journalistic muckraking has served to portray the plight of the elderly in institutional settings. Those fortunate enough to live in homes that provide social services and meaningful activity have some realistic hope of restoration. Institutions that make physical and occupational therapy available to those elderly who are recovering from illness or injury offer them considerable chance to return to a higher level of functioning. Those persons, however, who are exploited by false claims of rehabilitation and extended care in institutions have a greater likelihood of being left with a residual handicap and the subsequent need for a more structured, restricted form of living.

The sensory and interactional isolation suffered by many of the elderly in institutions results in what Stanly Cath calls "psychologically regressive and physiologically degenerative processes." Cath believes that, where persons fail to have meaningful object relationships, ego disorganization and a concomitant loosening of the chain of retrospective thought and fantasy may follow. Connections to the present seem lost. [13]

Older adults who are required to spend long periods of time in nursing homes and other settings away from their natural environment often display the following characteristic behaviors and attitudes: (1) Such individuals often become isolated and withdrawn in rooms and in wheelchairs. They may steer themselves into corners, preferring to remain in a state of self-absorption and despair over lost functioning. (2) They may be unable to cope with the variety of interpersonal demands in institutions, forgetting names, items of scheduled activities, and even normal social graces. (3) Their dress and grooming may deteriorate until they again can learn to take pride in the activities of daily living. (4) Previously independent persons may react to the rigid structure of the institution by demonstrating extreme dependence upon staff members. (5) Some may become openly hostile and suspicious of peers and staff. (6) Some may speak with uncertainty of their reality—of who they are, where they are, what their illnesses are, and where they are going. Butler believes that persons suffering from depression and anxiety—common emotional problems of the later years—can receive considerable relief. He extends hope for those with more severe functional disorders, even suggesting that persons with chronic brain syndromes or chronic physical illnesses can benefit from a variety of treatment modalities. [14]

Specialized Services: So What's New?

Out of our diverse, often complex planning structures throughout the country and, possibly, despite some planning efforts, a wide assortment of programs and services have been assembled in behalf of the elderly. How many of these have actually been conceived and implemented by the elderly themselves? There are no hard data available, but based on the recent pleas for consumer participation, it appears likely that a large percentage of current programs and services were created with little significant input from the elderly themselves. One of the newest innovations in the field is the inclusion of the elderly on planning commissions and on agency boards where policies are formulated.

Developmental Services

Developmental services are preventive in that they enable the elderly to maintain their personal and social well-being through the use of social-interactional, educational, and meaningful work activities.

Preretirement programs may be originated by union officials, union members, company officials, community agencies, recent retirees, or any number of agencies concerned with the elderly. Subjects for seminars sponsored by such programs include Social Security and Medicare; legal, financial, and housing problems; health and nutrition; consumer problems; use of leisure time; and volunteer activity.

Perhaps the most recognized form of developmental service to the elderly is the *senior citizens' center*. As early as 1953, Kubie and Landau vividly described their group work experiences in such an agency. [15] Through the years, centers have operated during the total week to provide a balanced schedule of social group work, recreation, and adult education. The emphasis has been on human relationships, whereby the elderly are helped to preserve their ability to function in the community and their horizons are broadened through virtually every conceivable form of activity. Ideally, such programs provide opportunities for passive or active participation, self-government, and continuing nourishment of special interest groups and club activities.

In recent years, these agencies have tended to provide more comprehensive programs and services; they may be designated as *multipurpose senior centers*. These centers frequently offer low-cost nutritional meals, public assistance services, Medicare and Medicaid advice, health screening, health maintenance, and, possibly, treatment clinics. The staff may offer information and referral service. The model center, as described by the National Council on Aging, includes social-recreational activities, adult education, arts and crafts, drama, music, dance, literary activities, a newspaper, nature study, sightseeing excursions, and camping vacations. It has various committees such as welcoming, public relations, hospitality, visiting, telephone reassurance, awards, grievance, history, house, and budget. More comprehensive centers may offer a barber shop/beauty parlor, clothing repair instruction, employment counseling, and housing programs.

Outreach activities to those persons who do not come to the center may be offered. "Reaching out" to the hard-to-reach elderly is being emphasized, particularly in view of the success of Project FIND. [16] The San Francisco Senior Center has successfully focused on such clients. [17]

Many community centers, settlement houses, park and recreation departments, and churches offer *senior citizens' clubs and groups*. While they are more limited in scope, they can supplement the activities of those elderly who are successfully meeting the challenge of growing old. Clubs and groups provide continuity in the lives of many older citizens.

Some communities enable the elderly to remain actively and meaningfully involved in their community through *volunteer services*. The Retired Senior Volunteer Program (RSVP), funded by ACTION, is a national program planned and operated at the local level. The elderly may volunteer as friendly visitors to homebound elderly, as teacher aides, as employment counselors, or as companions to institutionalized children.

Employment programs are beginning to gain wider acceptance. In South Carolina, for example, the State Employment Security Commission assists older persons to obtain jobs. Counseling, testing, and referral to training projects occur. Vocational rehabilitation offices serve the elderly just as they serve all persons with disabilities. Statistics for South Carolina offices in 1970-1971 showed that 227 persons over sixty-five years of age were placed in jobs.

The National Council on Aging has proposed a model community action program to employ older people as aides to work with children in general hospitals, preschool programs, schools for the mentally retarded, day camps, and church-supervised nurseries.[18] The Foster Grandparent Program has achieved widespread visibility in the past several years as a source of community service. Both the elderly poor and the children served have benefited from this imaginative program.

Educational Programs

Education for the aged is slowly becoming a developmental possibility. A thoughtful paper by Jeanne E. Bader shows that many colleges are welcoming older students and that the elderly want opportunities for continuing their education.[19] Some state universities are reaching out to the elderly via College Week Programs and free tuition arrangements.

Many library systems have received grants to purchase large-print books for elderly patrons with failing eyesight. Browsing collections of talking books are available in some libraries. The South Carolina-North Carolina regional library for the blind and handicapped provides talking books, record players and large-print books for those who qualify for the service.

Supportive Services

Supportive services are designed to forestall or prevent institutionalization by providing resources for maintaining the elderly person's ability to function more independently within the home and community.

Information and referral services have proven useful by increasing the elderly's awareness of existing services and by providing them with information pertinent to their needs. The elderly may secure information about food stamps, health care services, Social Security, nursing homes, and housing programs. The AoA currently considering the expanded use of telecommunications to improve awareness of existing services.

Legal services may include legal advice, routine litigation, test litigation, and possibly legislative and regulatory reform. Lawyers can be of service by developing strategies through which various needs may be met. For example, the elderly may need help in financial, nursing home, and landlord-tenant matters.

Health care services enable the elderly to make maximum use of health programs or to locate resources. The elderly need help in securing diagnostic, preventive, remedial, and related health services which are available through Medicare, Medicaid, or other agencies. Aside from help in the initial contact stage, the elderly may need assistance in carrying out medical recommendations, securing transportation, getting emergency aid, and, in some instances, obtaining bilingual interpreters. More attention should be focused on *health education* to insure that the aged will not only take advantage of services, but also get necessary immunizations. The elderly in particular need information about the physical activity and mobility essential to health maintenance. A remarkable outreach program of medical care for the elderly in high rise apartments has been sponsored by the University of Minnesota Medical School in cooperation with the Minneapolis Housing Authority. A dispensary within the apartment complex provides access to medical care for residents, thus making it unnecessary for them to leave their residence for medical service. Routine blood pressure checks, monitoring of reduction diets, foot care, refills of medications, as well as more thorough diagnostic and treatment services, are available in both the dispensary and, in some cases, the apartments. Special attention is given to elderly residents who have alcohol and drug abuse problems.

Home health care is an area where service gaps are often alarming and dangerous. Visiting nurses, home-health aides, geriatric aides, and other personnel are usually designated to provide a wide array of services such as preparing hot meals, shopping, giving personal care, doing light housework, and friendly visiting. The human contact they provide is essential for the elderly person who is temporarily homebound. Various program models also include such services as lawn care, snow removal, household repairs, escorting the elderly to medical care, and, in some communities, counseling.

The 1971 White House Conference on Aging recommended the development of homemaker-home health aid programs throughout the country—not just to serve the elderly, but the ill, disabled, children, and others as well. This form of service was termed an exemplary utilization of paraprofessional personnel. Foreseeing a wave of further action in this area, the conference also recommended the establishment of national standards to protect the quality of services rendered.

Foster care, a form of service well understood by social work personnel, is sometimes used as a form of noninstitutional care for the elderly. Under this service, care of the elderly is arranged in a private home wherein the owner-host maintains an active interest in the resident. Sometimes more than one person is placed in a single foster home. Some state mental hospitals use foster and boarding home plans as an alternative to further institutionalization of the elderly patient. Traditionally, social workers carefully select and supervise foster home placement.

Day hospitals and day care centers provide personal care and supervision to older persons with physical, mental, and social impairments. The opportunities they provide for social interaction, scheduled and open-ended program activities, social services, and the like may forestall institutionalization. Some elderly persons may enter day care and day hospital arrangements following a period of hospitalization. When multiservices are available, the family members may be more amenable to help care for elderly relatives. The day care arrangement minimizes the hazards of being home alone during the day, and the supportive relationships it provides may prevent deterioration and demoralization. *Vocational workshops* offer a potentially valuable resource for those elderly who might benefit from a structured work situation.

The Burke Rehabilitation Center Day Hospital in New York City, an outstanding model program, provides rehabilitation and psychosocial services to the aged who are chronically ill or disabled. Medical, dietary, counseling, occupational, physical and recreational therapy, and speech and hearing services are geared to the individual client for five to seven hours on a daily basis. Project Restore, part of the Tucson, Arizona, Model Cities Program, has operated a continuing day hospital program—one in a hospital and another in a nursing home. The state of Maryland has made impressive headway in creating this form of service.

Protective services are provided to elderly persons who are so mentally deteriorated or disturbed that they cannot manage their own affairs.[20] These persons usually have no relatives or friends who are able or willing to act in their behalf. Social work, legal, medical, psychiatric, community mental health outreach, homemaker, home health aide services, or any combination of these, may be utilized to enable the client to remain at home. If community services fail to achieve the prescribed objectives, total care in an institution may be necessary. At present, federal legislation permits local welfare departments to establish protective service programs for which the federal government provides up to 75 percent of the cost.

Telephone reassurance services for the homebound have achieved wider acceptance in the past few years. Community volunteers and the elderly themselves have contributed considerable time and effort to these services. Community agencies and churches often provide the funds or space needed to operate them. Services include information and referral. The elderly may request periodic reassurance calls to check on their well-being or merely to chat with another person. Friendly visitors, transportation and physical assistance, home maintenance, or counseling may also be requested. Miscellaneous services such as grocery delivery and talking books may be available.

An exciting therapeutic intervention program has recently been researched and described by Carol J. Barrett of the University of Southern California Andrus Gerontology Center and the Psychological Research and Service Center.[21] In a study dealing exclusively with widows, *group techniques* were developed to alleviate some of the stresses of these women. A self-help group, confidant group, and a woman's consciousness-raising group were experimentally studied over an eight-week period; depression was reduced in all groups. Following the research, each treatment group arranged continued contact. Barrett felt that all the group interventions showed potential in preventive mental health. The services can be designed to facilitate adjustment to widowhood and to reduce the sense of grief.

Within the immediate future, these various alternative services should be carefully evaluated. The feasibility and cost-effectiveness of alternative services are vital factors in considering changes in Medicare and Medicaid programs. The faster these programs can be evaluated, the faster we will be able to redefine our institutional provisions.

Services in Institutions

The issue of institutionalization of the elderly should diminish significantly in the near future as alternative programs and provisions requiring less than total supervision achieve more credibility. Agencies that provide restorative services will emerge in many communities to insure more efficient utilization of public and private funds for the elderly. For those who require institutional care, environmental conditions and social services will increasingly improve, thereby providing a more adequate quality of life for residents and patients. Butler's recent book on aging and mental health strongly suggests that positive psychosocial approaches to the care and treatment of the elderly are possible within institutional settings. [22]

In reality, effective social and physical rehabilitation programs are being planned and conducted throughout the country. The task ahead is to transmit knowledge on rehabilitation and total care to institutions that can put it to use. Institutions unable to make modern rehabilitative services operative should be cut off from public funding. More rigorous efforts must be made to upgrade standards of care and service. Activity program personnel must be trained and used to counteract the custodial-warehouse atmosphere of many institutions.

Several models of *group services* have been discussed in the recent literature. One work proposes a "system of groups" to provide residents of institutions with leisure-time pursuits through which they may assume personally satisfying life-roles. [23] A living and learning program for the elderly includes activity planning committees and self-management, special interest-skill mastery, creative activity, and enrichment groups. It is suggested that orientation groups can open channels of communication between residents and staff, promote the airing of feelings by residents and families, and set the stage for future problem-solving.

Moody, Baron, and Monk have described an imaginative use of the well-known *remotivation therapy* model in an extended care facility for the elderly. They investigated how professional nurses could enrich the sensory environment for older, immobilized patients. After several group sessions, the residents were more alert, had greater interest in life, and achieved better mood tones. This work affirms the belief that the aged can share a wealth of experiences and wisdom with others in groups. [24]

Reality orientation therapy is a technique for dealing with the confusion and disorientation usually associated with senility. The technique was conceived by Dr. James Folsom and introduced at the Tuscaloosa Veterans Administration Hospital in 1962. It promotes an around-the-clock orientation to the surrounding environment, with emphasis on time, place, and person. Thirty-minute class periods, five days a week, provide a structured set of activities to help the elderly. The hospital has conducted nationwide training of personnel for several years. [25] *Physical activities* may also be utilized with the elderly, not only to facilitate socialization with fellow patients, but also to enable patients to benefit from healthful exercise. [26]

Al Manaster, at the Parkview Home for the Aged in Chicago, reported in 1971 on the usefulness of *group therapy* with the "senile" patient. [27] He makes a cogent argument for using this technique on patients who have chronic brain syndrome. Sidney R. Shul and Shura Shul, at the Kingsbridge Heights Nursing Home in New York, suggest the value of enabling older people to discuss "death" in group psychotherapy sessions. They believe that healthy, open discussions alleviate some of the tension, ease depression, and help residents deal with death as another phase of life. [28]

The usefulness of the *therapeutic community* as a model of treatment of the elderly has been researched at Ypsilanti State Hospital in Michigan by the staff of the University of Michigan Institute of Gerontology. As reported by Dorothy Coons in 1973, elderly residents were exposed to a more humanistic approach to care. Social activities provided emotional contact, the physical environment was made more homelike, and opportunities for meaningful work were presented. Stimulation, responsibility, status, and rewards were advanced. Results of the project indicate improved self-image and levels of functioning in the residents. More importantly, the staff was more optimistic about the patients' ability to shed their institutional behavior. [29]

Social group work with families of the institutionalized aged has been successfully used at the Philadelphia Geriatric Center. As reported by Rotenberg and Rabin in 1973, time-limited group services were offered to families of physically impaired residents who were having the most overt difficulties in dealing with their parents' institutionalization. They were encouraged to speak openly of their feelings about the home and staff; the discussion moved toward common experiences of dealing with the parents' increasing demands and dependency, and the family's feelings of guilt and fear of the parents' death. [30] *Family group therapy* offered at the Parkview Home for the Aged in Chicago has similarly helped families achieve a more realistic acceptance of their parents and of themselves. The therapy has helped reduce anxieties, guilt, and fear, and it has increased appreciation for the problems of aging. [31] The supportive nature of group work suggests the need for further exploration and development of services to families of the elderly.

While *social work services* in residential institutions are achieving more acceptance by administrators and owners, implementation is not yet widespread. In 1974, a comprehensive guide to social work services in long-term care facilities was assembled by Elaine M. Brody.[32] The guide is intended to enable administrators, physicians, nurses, and other personnel to understand the potential of social work and to utilize it more fully. It describes services to applicants and families, services during the residence phase, discharge and aftercare services, services pertaining to death and dying, and social work with groups. The National Association of Social Workers completed a project in 1975 to train hundreds of social workers and social work designees employed in residential settings for the elderly. Social workers should be included on the residential staff to promote community placement of residents who no longer require the supportive environment of a restorative facility.

The Future

Many of the problems that continue to obstruct the emergence of community and institutional provisions for the elderly will diminish as our erroneous cultural assumptions about aging are corrected. Once the elderly themselves begin to organize and to emerge as a visible political force, we can expect a more rational sharing of professional resources and planning in their behalf. After a more enforceable system of accreditation for all levels of elderly care is devised, we can expect an upturn in the quality of care.

Notes

1. Marvin R. Koller, *Social Gerontology* (New York: Random House, 1968), p. 75.
2. Robert N. Butler, "Psychiatry and the Elderly: An Overview," *American Journal of Psychiatry* 312, No. 9 (September 1975): 894.
3. Michael Harrington, *The Other America: Poverty in the United States* (New York: Macmillan Co., 1962), pp. 101-120.
4. Claire Townsend, *Old Age: The Last Segregation* (New York: Grossman Co., 1971), p. x.
5. Elaine M. Brody, et al., "Excess Disabilities of Mentally Impaired Aged: Impact of Individualized Treatment," *The Gerontologist* (Summer 1971): 124-133.
6. Wilbur J. Cohen, "The Challenge of Aging," Paper supplied by the author, no date given.
7. 1971 White House Conference on Aging, *Section Recommendations on Planning* (Washington, D.C.: U.S. Government Printing Office, 1971).
8. Administration on Aging, *Research and Development Strategy* (Washington, D.C.: Office of Human Development, U.S. Department of Health, Education, and Welfare, 1975), p. 59.
9. 1971 White House Conference on Aging, *Planning: Background and Issues* (Washington, D.C.: U.S. Government Printing Office, 1971), p. 35.
10. Ibid., p. 17.
11. Ibid.
12. Jean M. Maxwell, "Group Services: Well-Being for Older People," in *Social Work with Groups, 1960: Selected Papers from the National Conference on Social Welfare* (New York: National Association of Social Workers, 1960), pp. 78-79.
13. Stanley H. Cath, "Some Dynamics of Middle and Later Years," *Smith College Studies in Social Work* 33 (February 1963): 121.
14. Butler, op. cit., p. 895.

15. Susan H. Kubie and Gertrude Landau, *Group Work with the Aged* (New York: International Universities Press, 1953).

16. National Council on Aging, *The Golden Years: A Tarnished Myth* (Washington, D.C.: Office of Economic Opportunity, 1970).

17. F. Estelle Booth, *Reaching Out to the Hard-to-Reach Older Person* (San Francisco: San Francisco Senior Center, 1967).

18. National Council on Aging, *Tender Loving Care* (Washington, D.C.: Office of Economic Opportunity, 1965).

19. Jeanne E. Bader, "Education for Older Adults: A Review of the Literature, Some Commendations, and Some Predictions," Paper presented at the annual meeting of the Gerontological Society, Miami Beach, 1973.

20. Group for the Advancement of Psychiatry, *The Aged and Community Mental Health: A Guide to Program Development* (New York: 1971), pp. 74-75.

21. Carol J. Barrett, "A Comparison of Therapeutic Interventions with Widows," Paper presented at the annual meeting of the Gerontological Society, Miami Beach, 1973.

22. Robert N. Butler and Myrna I. Lewis, *Aging and Mental Health* (St. Louis: C. V. Mosby Co., 1973), pp. 208-246.

23. Gerald L. Euster, "A System of Groups in Institutions for the Aged," *Social Casework* 52, No. 8 (October 1971): 523-529.

24. Linda Moody, et al., "Moving the Past into the Present," *American Journal of Nursing* 70, No. 11 (November 1970): 2253-2256.

25. Robert J. Trotter, "Reality Orientation," *Science News* (December 1972): 411.

26. Richard L. Comstick, "Simple Physical Activities for the Elderly," *Hospital and Community Psychiatry* (December 1969): 377-380.

27. Al Manaster, "Therapy with the 'Senile' Geriatric Patient," Paper read at the annual conference, American Group Psychotherapy Association, 1971.

28. Sidney R. Shul and Shura Shul, "Old People Talk About Death," *OMEGA* 4, No. 1 (1973): 27-35.

29. Dorothy H. Coons, "Developing a Therapeutic Community: Impact of Research on an Empirical Model and Staff Training Materials," Paper presented at the annual meeting of the Gerontological Society, Miami Beach, 1973.

30. Sandra E. Rotenberg and Joy S. Rabin, "Social Group Work with Families of Institutionalized Aged," Paper presented at the annual meeting of the Gerontological Society, Miami Beach, 1973.

31. Al Manaster, "The Family Group Therapy Program at Parkview Home for the Aged," *Journal of the American Geriatrics Society* 15, No. 3 (March 1967): 302-306.

32. Elaine M. Brody, *A Social Work Guide for Long-Term Care Facilities* (Washington, D.C.: National Institute of Mental Health, 1974).

6
IMPLEMENTING A TITLE VII NUTRITIONAL PROGRAM

Lillian Colby, Carol Hill, Nancy Derrington, and Deborah Tyra

Orientation to Title VII

On October 31, 1972, throughout the state of Alabama, six Title III Area-wide Model Project applications on aging were submitted to the Alabama State Commission on Aging. The purpose of these applications was to develop comprehensive plans of action for target groups of older persons in Alabama who were in danger of being institutionalized for the lack of services being provided. This plan was the base from which, in 1973, the Title VII nutrition program for the elderly, Public Law 92-258, was developed for Alabama. In 1973, the six Areawide Model Projects were designated area agencies on aging (AAAs). Planning and administration of Title VII nutrition programs were designed to parallel and complement existing Title III programs in order to insure a total, comprehensive aging initiative.

Planning Areas

Alabama is divided into substate planning and service areas (PSAs). These consist of groups of local governments within each area, i.e., counties, cities, and towns, which may join voluntarily, but must join to be eligible for certain funding. There are twelve PSAs, ten of which have been designated for priority development. One of these areas comprises the West Alabama Planning and Development Council (WAPDC).

Title VII Criteria

The general criteria for Title VII nutrition project plans are as follows:
Resources: Because of relatively limited resources, each nutrition project had to be developed as a comprehensive program. The unit cost for each meal, with the necessary supportive social services, had to be kept as low as possible. At the same time, the project had to have a maximum positive impact on the lives of older persons.

Overhead: A relatively high "overhead" cost was to be allowed for each nutrition project. This would allow each AAA to plan, develop, and assume responsibility for all nutrition and allied supportive services to be delivered to the target population within the given PSA. Therefore, the nutrition program as operated in Alabama was developed as a series of small, isolated projects with a single nutrition project established in each of six PSAs. Under the administrative structure of a single statewide Title VII nutrition project, a number of congregate meal sites were established within each project area.

AAA Coordination: To further reduce the unit cost of each meal and to provide a coordinated, integrated approach with maximum utilization of existing resources, each AAA was expected to assist in the planning, development, coordination, management, and evaluation of nutrition services within its area of responsibility.

Minimum Number of Meals: In all instances, area nutrition projects would serve no less than the required minimum of 100 meals, five days a week. Insofar as possible, the projects would also be developed on an areawide basis, the minimum number of meals ranging from 300 for rural PSAs to over 1,000 for urban PSAs.

Multiple Sites: Since it would not be feasible to operate areawide nutrition projects with only one or two nutrition sites, each project would consist of a central coordinating agency with multiple feeding sites. Sites would have to be accessible to areas and neighborhoods with a large porportion of the designated target population.

Survey: Before the nutrition program could be established, a survey of the needs of older adults was to be conducted. This was one of the specific guidelines for implementation established by the Older Americans Act of 1965, amended in 1972. This survey could be contracted to another agency or undertaken by the AAAs. Throughout the state different modes were used to conduct the survey. The WAPDC contracted its survey to the Center for the Study of Aging, University of Alabama School of Social Work. The survey was conducted in March 1973 and included 2,000 older persons living in a seven-county area. Prior to this survey, an article explaining the project was published in all county and city newspapers in west Alabama.

Proposals: Prior to receiving funding for the Title VII nutrition project, the applicant agencies submitted proposals for a nutrition project award. The provisions outlined in the proposal would become part of the official application and would therefore be binding upon the conduct of the project subsequent to the award of any funds by the state agency.

Subcontracts: The AAAs implementing Title VII projects for social services, including transportation, outreach, and escort services, could enter into subcontracts with public or private nonprofit agencies. The purpose would be to meet the social needs of older persons on a countywide basis. The WAPDC would be responsible for carrying out the objectives of the nutrition program, coordinating the program, and selecting agencies to administer the subcontracts. An appropriate number of subcontracts would be given to minority organizations to comply with federal regulations.

Jurisdiction: Agencies applying for subcontracts were required to certify that their Title VII Nutrition Project award proposals had been submitted for comment to the AAA that had jurisdiction over the proposed project area. The prospective grantee agency also had to agree to the following contractual stipulations:

1. That the project be carried out in accordance with Title VII of the Older Americans Act, the program regulations issued thereto, the policies and procedures established by the state agency for the nutrition program, and the terms and conditions as approved by the state agency in making any award of funds.

2. That the project cooperate in joint planning with existing or local agencies responsible for comprehensive planning in aging in the proposed project area and with the providers of services to the aging in the area in order to make additional services available to project participants.

3. That the project provide for the training necessary to enable paid and volunteer project personnel to administer the project.

4. That the project cooperate and assist in all state agency or Administration on Aging (AoA) efforts to evaluate the effectiveness, feasibility, and costs of the project.

5. That more than half the membership of the nutrition project council be actual consumers of the project's nutrition services and be representative of individuals at the congregate meal sites. That the operations of the nutrition project council be carried out in accordance with the policies and procedures established by the state agency.

6. That no personal information obtained from an individual in conjunction with the project be identified with that person without his written consent.

7. That records be kept and reports made as required by the state agency and in accordance with AoA guidelines.

8. That the project comply with all applicable state and local standards, including fire, health, safety, and sanitation, prescribed in law or regulations.

9. That such accounts and documents be maintained so as to permit expeditious determination of the status of funds within the award.

10. That the project comply with Title VI of the Civil Rights Act of 1964 (Public Law 88-352).

In most cases, interagency cooperation has been accomplished through written letters of agreement or of understanding specifically stating a service agency's plan for providing input to AAA programs. For example, many social service agencies simply state that they agree to provide a stipulated number of programs to nutrition site participants throughout the year. If written documentation is not feasible, the AAA and the service agency involved can make verbal agreements. In cases where there is a state agreement between the State Commission on Aging and a state service agency, such as the Department of

Public Health, the informal understanding serves at the local level to reinforce the statewide agreement.

Services Provided

Any complete Title VII nutrition program is required to offer a variety of supportive social services to each program participant. These include transportation, escort, information and referral, nutrition education, health and welfare counseling, shopping assistance, consumer education, and recreation. In each year of the nutrition program, changes in the planning and implementation of the program have been made as the clients' needs have changed and as resources available to programs serving older Americans have increased.

Transportation and *escort services* have been provided both by contracting and subcontracting agencies. Participants are taken to and from their homes, to and from nutrition sites, to recreational activities, and to other service agencies.

Major social service agencies since 1973 have provided many supportive services. *Information and referral* (I&R) has been and will continue to be provided to nutrition project participants by the Department of Social Security, Food Stamp Office, and Department of Pensions and Security. The Farmers Home Administration, Alabama Power Company, Alabama Gas Corporation, and West Alabama Rehabilitation Services, as well as small local contracting agencies, also provide I&R. Other I&R services have been provided by information directories published by the various planning commissions. When the occasion arises, site managers themselves provide this necessary service.

The staff of the County Extension Office provides *nutrition education* bimonthly. *Nutrition Education Comments*, a newsletter published by the Auburn University nutritionist under contract with the Alabama State Commission on Aging, is distributed as an information resource at many nutrition sites.

Health and welfare counseling is provided not only by the County Health Departments but also by the local fire department, police department, and local businesses such as drug stores whose personnel visit nutrition sites. Other health and welfare counseling is done by persons representing the County Extension Offices and by films on health.

In the past, *shopping assistance* has been furnished through such activities as local grocery store workers teaching comparative shopping. Sales papers from these local grocery stores are provided on a regular basis by site managers at many of the nutrition sites. Shopping information is made available to the site as it is received by the nutrition project director. Shopping assistance may also take the form of trips to local grocery stores and shopping centers.

Consumer education in the areas of grocery shopping, health foods, and other nutritional supplements has been presented via films and a weekly newsletter published by the Governor's Office of Consumer Protection and mailed directly to site managers.

Recreation service is the primary responsibility of the site managers. Recreation includes singing, games, quilting, films, visiting choirs, arts and crafts, parties, and hobby shows. During the summer months, the site participants frequently order a special picnic lunch instead of the regular lunch, and they visit one of the nearby scenic lakes or other picnic areas. Other recreational activities include visits to libraries, fashion shows, bands, and skits presented by children from local schools and churches. Sometimes the participants themselves entertain, such as by holding a bluegrass "picking and singing" or by reciting poetry. Photographs of the activities are taken and displayed on posters. The AAA staff also encourages all participants to enter exhibits in local displays and fairs.

A Title VII Program Implementation

The actual operation of a nutrition program in Tuscaloosa County will be considered here. Although this county is classified as rural, of the 116,029 persons counted in the 1970 Census, 79 percent lived within the city of Tuscaloosa and the remaining 21 percent in Northport (a separate incorporated city divided from Tuscaloosa only by the Warrior River) and in the surrounding 1,340 square-mile county area (second largest in the state). Nationally, persons over sixty years of age comprise approximately 10 percent of the population, but in Tuscaloosa County 13 percent (15,512 people) are in this age group.

The survey by the University of Alabama School of Social Work cited previously indicated the need for at least two congregate meal sites for the program. While the nutrition program considers all persons to be eligible participants, a very large number of low-income people over sixty years of age were found in two of the federal housing projects within the city of Tuscaloosa. This high concentration made these locations logical centers for reaching older persons with the special problems of limited incomes, marginal health, and limited transportation resources.

WAPDC made the initial plans and contacts for implementing the program. The director of the Tuscaloosa Housing Authority and its governing board agreed to allow the nutrition program to operate in the two housing projects, McKenzie and Rosedale Courts. They generously underwrote the extensive renovation and modernization of kitchen facilities at each site to bring them into compliance with Health Department regulations. In addition, as a direct result of the interest of nutrition participants at McKenzie Court, the oldest housing project in the city, a long-planned remodeling and redecorating of the auditorium was undertaken. The reopening and rededication of the extremely attractive new facilities took place in conjunction with the nutrition program.

WAPDC also hired one manager for each site. The managers were to work four hours a day, five days a week. Among their duties were to care for the site; receive the prepared food; organize volunteer help to prepare the site, serve meals, and clean up; maintain reports as required by WAPDC and state and federal authorities; and help plan and carry out recreational and educational programs.

FOCUS

During the months of planning prior to the November 1973 opening of the sites, WAPDC personnel consulted with the newly activated countywide co-ordinating agency for programs for the aging, FOCUS on Senior Citizens of Tuscaloosa County, a nonprofit, private agency. The executive director of FOCUS made arrangements for bringing undergraduate seniors and graduate students from the University of Alabama School of Social Work into active participation in the program. The activities of these studies in the early phase of the program will be discussed later.

FOCUS also contributed to the original planning activities through its federally funded Retired Senior Volunteer Program (RSVP). The RSVP director recruited and trained the volunteers, who continue to provide the basic house-keeping services for the nutrition sites—the backbone of the nutrition program. By encouraging older persons to volunteer, many additional benefits have resulted. The volunteers also receive the benefits of the meals and the auxiliary nutrition program services. The other participants feel a kinship with the workers and vice-versa. The volunteers can alert the staff to additional potential participants; foresee occasional problems and frequently suggest solutions; and provide psychological and social insights that younger persons could not be expected to have. Finally, the volunteers can receive the additional benefits built into the ACTION-RSVP framework.

The nutrition program was inaugurated in November 1973, with appropriate ceremonies involving the State Commission on Aging and various elected officials in the area. Two months later, WAPDC entered into contract with FOCUS to take over management of the two sites. That agency has held the contract since then, but the two original state managers have remained. The School of Social Work has continued to place students at the sites and has provided full-time field education supervisors in compliance with university and accrediting agency policies.

The FOCUS director is the liaison between the nutrition sites and area and state agencies; plans and obtains some of the educational and social programs; performs normal managerial and supervisory functions; and carries out provisions of the Title VII contract. No serious problems connected with the operation of the sites have occurred other than occasional communication and minor administrative problems and some personality conflicts, all of which have either been resolved or ameliorated.

FOCUS has also contributed support through its service component, Seniors on the Move. For the first ten months of the nutrition program, participation was limited to those who lived within walking distance of the sites or who had their own transportation or access to friends' vehicles. (The local public transportation system is not flexible enough to meet the special needs of older persons). In July 1974, FOCUS received a contract to provide I&R and linkage services. With the inception of door-to-door service by two minibuses made possible by this contract, persons could be brought from outlying areas to the sites. As a consequence, twenty to twenty-five individuals can now participate at least once or twice a week. Rides have also been furnished to special events.

The Social Work Students

During each semester of the university academic year four to eight students are placed in the nutrition program. In the course of translating their classroom learning into practical terms, they have conducted the initial outreach to recruit participants for the program; taken individual clients to the University of Alabama Medical School in Birmingham for specialized treatment; planned craft fairs; identified clients' needs for protective services; written an annotated local resource directory; participated in FOCUS staff meetings; organized sightseeing and picnic trips; initiated educational programs; given comfort and support to dying clients; organized and supported advisory committees at each site; and rescued a client from eviction proceedings and provided for his treatment for alcoholism and eventual rehabilitation.

One program headed by the students provided the advice, organization, and "legwork" for compiling the favorite recipies of nutrition participants and publishing them in a moneymaking cookbook. The money derived from sales is being used to finance social activities and sightseeing trips.

Another program was a fashion show where men and women modeled outfits that they themselves had designed. With the help of a student placed with the Parks and Recreation Authority, the social work students recruited the models and interviewed them regarding the outfits they planned to wear, their special points of interest, and the reasons for their choices. This information was then written up and presented in typical "fashion show" style. This type of program has since been successfully repeated at an RSVP party and at a communitywide Senior Citizens' Day. It is a useful alternative to the sometimes financially and stylistically unrealistic shows produced commercially.

For many students, work with the elderly has been a meaningful and long-lasting experience. Some have kept in touch with their former clients or have continued to visit the sites long after their academic work was completed.

With the cooperation of faculty from the School of Social Work, the FOCUS director developed a self-evaluation guide. It parallels and elaborates on the student evaluation form that supervisors complete for each student at the end of a field education experience. The guide is designed as a learning tool for the students; they are encouraged to keep a copy for their personal files and are required to turn in either a narrative or item-answered paper. Students are advised to use the self-evaluation as a means of measuring how their field experience has contributed to their growth in knowledge and understanding.

Most evaluations submitted each semester have shown a serious commitment and real developmental change as a result of field experience.

WAPDC Contributions

All of the educational and recreational programs mentioned here have been carried out at the two Tuscaloosa sites; many were initiated there and were later copied in other counties. Similarly, suggestions from the other areas have been adapted for use locally.

The local implementation of three project ideas originating with the WAPDC staff is especially notable. The first of these was the Disaster Relief Plan. Based on experience gained by the WAPDC when a tornado struck in several densely populated areas with large concentrations of older persons, the FOCUS staff drew up a detailed disaster plan and distributed copies to each staff member and to the School of Social Work. After submission to the FOCUS board of directors, the plan was delivered to the Tuscaloosa County Civil Defense director. The phone numbers of key FOCUS staff were included in the cover letter to Civil Defense. Each FOCUS staff person has an up-to-date telephone list of all Civil Defense and service agency staff, so that in the event of a disaster resources can be mobilized quickly.

The second useful idea originating from WAPDC was the institution of the annual Appreciation Day. On this occasion, all agencies, businesses, and individuals who have contributed to the educational or recreational aspects of the nutrition program are given certificates of appreciation signed by the chairman of WAPDC and its executive director. Each certificate is inscribed with the name of the honoree and is personally presented by the director. The certificates are now being used in each of the seven counties participating in the Title VII program. The recipients appear genuinely pleased to be so recognized, and it is felt that Appreciation Day has been a valuable public relations tool.

The third creative program idea was the celebration of the completion of a full-year of program operation. Many of the officials present at the opening returned for the anniversary. Certificates and commemorative buttons were presented to volunteers who had participated for a full year. Again, this "official" recognition proved an excellent morale booster.

Program Evaluation

To date, 400 persons have participated in Tuscaloosa's nutrition program. Currently, there are 250 people on the active rolls. While probably 75 percent have incomes below the poverty line, some are financially comfortable (those who have part-time employment or independent incomes). The roster includes retired school principals, carpenters, and domestics, as well as many who have never held jobs. Between 80 and 100 persons are served daily (the number has fluctuated from 75 to 120, depending on the weather or other conditions). Some people participate every day, while others attend only once or twice a week. This may be only a small percentage of the target population, but even so, these people have benefited from the socialization and the psychological and financial support provided by the program. Through association with the program, the lives of many have been radically altered for the better, as evidenced by behavioral and physical changes, some of which have been quite dramatic.

Toward the end of the first year, the university students analyzed the impact of the program on the clients they had worked with during one semester. Out of 150 persons, they identified fifteen who had been close to needing referral to nursing homes at the time they began working with them. Directly through receiving wholesome, nutritious food and indirectly through the supportive services initiated by student and staff intervention, these fifteen people were able to maintain an independent living. The financial savings in terms of taxpayers' dollars *not* spent for nursing home costs was $65,000; the human savings in terms of personal happiness and independence cannot be calculated.

PART III
Volunteerism and Aging—
The ACTION Family

7

VOLUNTEER SERVICES RENDERED BY THE AGING

Catherine B. Healy

Volunteerism is viewed here not only in terms of the contributions of the elderly to the field, but also as a rehabilitative process for older people. In addition, the role of ACTION, the federal agency for volunteer programs, in providing the aging with this rehabilitative opportunity is discussed.

Programs Under ACTION

Congress designated ACTION as the vehicle for forging "an alliance of the generations" through volunteer service to all who need help at home and abroad. Created under the Reorganization Plan No. 1 of 1971, ACTION brought together volunteer programs heretofore scattered throughout the federal system, namely, the Peace Corps; VISTA (Volunteers in Service to America); the University Year for Action, which offers opportunities for college students to become involved in community service; and the Foster Grandparent Program, the Senior Companion Program, and the Retired Senior Volunteer Program, all three of which offer specific voluntary opportunities, especially for older Americans, to share their time, talents, and skills in community service.

Under the direction of ACTION, each of these volunteer programs has retained its own identity and unique purpose, while at the same time building on the strengths and experiences of the others. Over the past three years, these volunteer programs together have fostered not only their own individual efforts, but citizen involvement in community service as well. At the present time, 150,000 full- and part-time volunteers are working in the various ACTION programs. Under the mandates of legislation signed by President Nixon on October 1, 1973, ACTION has been designated the national focal point for citizen service, providing both younger and older Americans the opportunity to perform meaningful volunteer service.

The Peace Corps

Since its inception in 1961, many senior citizens have joined the Peace Corps, helping people in fifty-six developing countries to improve their life and living standards. The main requirements for Peace Corps service are that the volunteer be an American citizen and eighteen years of age or older. There is no upper age limit, and a growing number of older persons, many of them retired, are volunteering. Peace Corps volunteers live at the level of the people with whom they work, learning the language and culture and sharing knowledge and skills. This is basic to the Peace Corps philosophy and the primary reason for its success.

VISTA

VISTA is the domestic counterpart of the Peace Corps. In every training cycle for VISTA, a substantial number of older Americans have joined forces with younger people to work in poverty areas. VISTA volunteers live and work among the poor, the disadvantaged, and the neglected in the United States. They serve as catalysts in the community and help the poor to develop self-help skills. Many VISTA volunteers are older local residents of the community in which they serve. Following completion of training and assignment to a project, they commit themselves to a calendar year of full-time service. Projects may be sponsored by a variety of public or private nonprofit organizations. The prime requirements for joining VISTA are that the volunteers be citizens of the United States or one of its territories, and that they have the desire to serve, the emotional and physical strength required for sensitive and difficult work, the willingness to learn, the patience to persist despite frustrations, and the capacity to give needed assistance to local community leaders.

Volunteer Programs for Older Americans

The Foster Grandparent, Senior Companion, and Retired Senior Volunteer Programs were designed specifically to involve capable and available older persons in community service, to offer them the opportunity to remain a viable force in their communities, and to give them the self-respect and satisfaction that comes from being needed and serving others.

In today's rapidly changing world, youth tend not to listen to "the way it was" or to see the value of "how it used to be." They do not appreciate the fact that the senior citizen of today has mastered more changes than any single generation in history and has learned about survival through three-quarters of a century of unprecedented change. Margaret Mead reminds us that the aged know something that youth need to know. They are knowledgeable in ways that we have not yet learned to ask or they to teach. One of the primary recommendations of the 1971 White House Conference on Aging was to develop programs for older Americans which would utilize the experience, knowledge, and skills of the elderly. These three volunteer programs are designed for this purpose.

The Foster Grandparent Program was established in 1965 and was formerly part of the Administration on Aging in the Department of Health, Education, and Welfare. Now one of the ACTION programs, it provides part-time volunteer opportunities for low-income persons aged sixty or over, and person-to-person service to children with special needs. The goals of the program are to involve capable older persons in productive service, to enable them to remain active, to give them a voice in their communities, and to foster their self-respect.

The Retired Senior Volunteer Program (RSVP) was authorized by the 1969 amendments to the Older Americans Act. It offers men and women, aged sixty and over, new and varied opportunities for volunteer service in their communities. Federal grants are available for these programs, but applicant agencies and organizations must present a plan for continuing the nonfederal contributions before any federal money can be awarded. These programs are designed to be organized and operated by local public or private nonprofit organizations based in the local communities involved. Through RSVP, older persons serve in schools, parks, courts, museums, day care centers, hospitals, libraries, welfare agencies, and nursing homes. Assignments are matched to the needs of the volunteer as well as the organization. RSVP volunteers receive no compensation but are reimbursed for out-of-pocket expenses.

The Senior Companion Program is the newest of ACTION's volunteer programs for older Americans. It provides part-time volunteer opportunities for low-income persons, sixty years of age or older. Its major purpose is to provide person-to-person service to adults with special or exceptional needs in health, education, welfare, and related settings.

Volunteer Benefits of ACTION Programs

The 1971 White House Conference on Aging stressed that older persons need to have satisfying and useful activity and that they should be assisted in remaining in their own homes in order to delay or prevent institutionalization. In his message to Congress, President Nixon asked Congress to "authorize the ACTION agency to expand person-to-person volunteer service programs, helping older Americans to work both with children and with older persons." As a result, the Older American Comprehensive Services Amendments of 1973 were passed in May of that year (Public Law 93-29). The current authority is Title II, Part B, of the Domestic Volunteer Services Act of 1973.

These programs have shown that most aging persons can function fairly well in their daily living. Even though aging does slow down the mental and physical processes, older volunteers can still perform a wide variety of activities, both in the home and in the community. Older people begin to have problems of functioning when they retire and find themselves with endless hours of unplanned-for leisure and reduced family responsibilities. With job and family responsibilities complete, it is the rare older person who can retain his self-esteem and position of social or community importance. If left to their own devices, few people truly find satisfaction in their later years.

Countless services have been created *for* the aging, but community services through the ACTION volunteer programs constitute one of the first efforts to create services *with* the aging. ACTION volunteer programs are specifically designed to offer the older person a "second time around": a status position in the community through board and committee work, dignity and respect through service, and satisfaction through being needed and performing a necessary job.

Older persons cannot be regarded as a homogeneous group. As in any age group, each is an individual with his own distinct attitudes and desires and his own right of self-determination within his own physical and mental limits. The ACTION programs are designed to accommodate these individual differences and to provide wide choices of service for each person. Volunteerism is a very personal matter, which begins with a personal commitment by the volunteer to "give himself" and which moves on to the giving of one's self to someone or something. Experience has shown that to involve older persons in the giving of themselves in community service significantly contributes to their physical and mental well-being.

Several interesting studies have been done recently on the attitudes and behavior patterns of older persons involved in volunteer service. One finding was that older volunteers have much better attendance and retention records than younger volunteers. In general, older volunteers tend to be on time for their assignment and are seldom absent because of illness. One hospital administrator reported that the turnover rate for the paid staff was 30 percent, while that for the senior volunteers was only 1 percent.

Older volunteers like to move quickly into their assignments and often become deeply involved with the task they are performing. For many, the volunteer service is the highlight of the week, and the patient or client receiving the service becomes the focal point of their lives. As one eighty-two-year-old volunteer puts it, "My arthritis never seems to bother me on Thursday when I come to the hospital to read to Mary."

The older volunteer needs a variety of choices of volunteer assignments in order to find the one that he will feel most comfortable doing. In other words, each assignment must be individualized to maximize the volunteer's potential. Often, surprising new talents are discovered, and the older volunteer gains satisfaction from realizing that he can learn "new tricks." In one medical setting in Kentucky, Foster Grandparents have become a vital part of the diagnostic team that studies and evaluates handicapped children. The volunteers give supportive services upon the recommendations of the professional evaluation team. For example, they repeatedly offer a toy to handicapped children to help build their grasping reflexes, or they massage twisted limbs, or they get on the floor to help a child learn to crawl. These volunteer services are very important to older people. As one Foster Grandparent stated: "I'd rather go on bread and water than to do without 'my child'; he loves me and I love him and I can't wait each day to see him and take him a surprise. My life is no longer lonely; when I go home I am never lonely, for I am thinking, planning and fixing a surprise for the next visit. In the morning I don't ache any more, suddenly, I am not old anymore."

In June 1971, the Department of Health, Education, and Welfare contracted with the Booze-Allen Public Administration Sevice to conduct a cost-benefit study of the Foster Grandparent Program. The results of the study show that older volunteers are motivated by their desires to help others, particularly children, and to lose their feelings of loneliness, pain, and uselessness. Some 75 percent of Foster Grandparents interviewed reported their volunteer work was one of their most enjoyable experiences in the past five years.

The unusual aspect of the Foster Grandparent Program is that it is of enormous benefit to both the doer and the recipient. For the children, the kindness, patience, and love that they receive improve their lives. In many cases, the children served show improvement in their physical, social, and psychological development. In some cases, the individual attention that each older volunteer gives each child results in early release of the child from the institution or the early termination of costly special treatment. Many institutional administrators and grantee agencies also point out that volunteer participation improves the community image of the agency.

The Booze-Allen report concludes that society-at-large receives great benefits from these volunteer programs. In return for providing tax dollars for program funds, society receives the benefit of improving the economic and social well-being of older Americans, which in turn contributes to their future independence.

ACTION is expanding volunteer service opportunities for persons of all ages. It is also striving to increase the effectiveness of volunteer programs in dealing with social problems. ACTION is trying new and innovative approaches to voluntary service in an attempt to meet the challenges of the 1970s. Older persons have contributed to the mental health and well-being of all older Americans through their spirited participation in volunteer programs and continuing adjustments to a rapidly changing world:

> Psychologists, politicians, and others who should know better are writing books, making speeches and pressuring Congress regarding the problems of these poor "unfortunates." This is like trying to teach a fish how to swim. These poor "unfortunates" in their lifetime have adjusted to the Depression, the TVA, WPA, NRA and Social Security, to the 40-hour week, to labor unions, to civil rights riots and to space exploration.

> They've progressed from oil lamps to electricity, from gramophones

to televisions, from ice boxes to home freezers, from wood stoves to gas, from pasteboard fans to air conditioning, from high button shoes to sandals, from stairs to automatic elevators, from change drawers to cash registers, from hand cranked cars to automatic transmissions.

As one active participant noted: "Heck, anyone who is retiring at sixty-five these days is an old hand at making adjustments and could probably tell the young upstarts a few things! Some of them can't even adjust from college to employment or unemployment."

8
THE RETIRED SENIOR VOLUNTEER PROGRAM

Amelia B. Heath

The local development of an ACTION program such as the Retired Senior Volunteer Program (RSVP) is a slow process. The federal guidelines spell out a detailed procedure for implementation, and many steps must be taken to reach the goal of an established, viable program. Local sponsorship and direction are essential since communities vary greatly.

The implementation described here occurred in a small southern town located in a largely rural county comprising 116,000 persons. The population is heaviest in the center of the county, with 81 percent of the people living within a ten-mile radius. The remainder are scattered over an area approximately fifty-five by fifty miles. A total of 15,613 residents are over sixty years of age, of whom 3,479 are black, 3,726 have incomes below the poverty level, and 2,226 live alone. A large majority of older persons live in individual rather than congregate housing.

RSVP Organization

The successful RSVP requires the selection of the most appropriate and interested sponsor. The Tuscaloosa program began in late 1971 when a program development specialist of the state unit on aging approached a committee of citizens interested in services for older adults. The specialist explained the details of the new federally funded ACTION program, RSVP. The committee members, later to become FOCUS on Senior Citizens, then wrote a grant proposal to ACTION. The staff members of the Alabama State Commission on Aging supplied guidelines, a suggested format, and ongoing assistance. In the initial planning stage, the community's need for the program had to be clearly established. Committee members informed agency representatives in the fields of aging, volunteerism, and social services of the programmatic aspects of RSVP, and they requested permission to confirm, by letter, the need for the program as a resource for the aged and as a source of volunteers for community agencies.

This initial step was an assurance that the program would be geared to community preferences, and it took into account the varying service groups already in the community. This community involvement procedure was necessary since many federally funded programs have previously failed to integrate themselves into the community and, therefore, have not succeeded in serving the citizens on a long-range basis.

Just prior to and concurrent with work on the RSVP grant application, the citizens' committee took steps to formalize itself into a nonprofit private agency. Funding for the agency was secured from the Tuscaloosa County Commission. By 1972, the parent agency and its first program, RSVP, were begun.

While federal guidelines suggest that an advisory committee be appointed and participate in the early stages of an RSVP, none was appointed in Tuscaloosa until after the grant had been awarded because the parent agency was being organized at the same time. The committee was structured according to ACTION guidelines and included persons representing volunteerism in the community—experts in aging, representatives from senior groups, and members of the business community and local government. The original committee was composed of the state coordinator of the American Association of Retired Persons; the district coordinator of the National Retired Teachers Association; a retired school principal; a retired college professor; a retired engineer; a retired insurance man; the chief of volunteer services at the Veterans Administration Hospital; the coordinator of the Voluntary Action Center; older persons extremely active in voluntary service; a representative from the local area agency on aging; two persons from the FOCUS board of directors; a businessman who is also a retired legislator; a banker; an employee of the Social Security Administration Office; and the director of the County Extension Service. People sixty years of age and over, some of them program participants, made up a minimum of 25 percent of the committee. Approximately the same membership has been maintained.

Program Funding

Actual implementation of a program begins when the RSVP grant is awarded. ACTION allocates funds to the grantee on a quarterly basis. After the notice of the grant award is received, the initial quarterly installment is sent to the board of directors and is then transferred to the RSVP. Continued funding is obtained by quarterly requests, which are processed through ACTION's state and regional offices one month prior to the end of each quarter. Funds are forwarded to each grantee just before the start of the quarter. Following each quarter, a financial statement report, prepared on forms supplied by ACTION, is made. This report is prepared by the RSVP staff, but it is reviewed and signed by the president of the board of directors of the grantee agency since fiscal responsibility for the program lies with that body.

While program plans are developed on a five-year basis, they are not automatically renewable but are subject to annual review and evaluation. Congress has built in an escalating local support factor of 10 percent of the total budget for the first year, 20 percent for the second, 30 percent for the third, 40 percent for the fourth, and 50 percent for the fifth. After five years, the grant will continue at 50 percent local matching funds and 50 percent federal funds, contingent upon acceptance of the yearly grant renewal application, which must detail current program activities and proposed plans for the coming year. Each application for renewal must include an itemized budget reflecting both federal and nonfederal support of the program. This budget is prepared ninety days in advance of the end of the budget year and is sent to ACTION regional and state offices and to the state unit on aging.

The grant application must be approved by the president of the board of directors before it can be mailed. Before the end of the forty-five-day review period, a field representative of ACTION visits the program and may make suggestions for changes in the application. Final approval for the succeeding year's grant must be made within forty days. This required process insures that a program undergoes a thorough review; permits a reevaluation of goals, objectives, and budgets; and provides for a thorough assessment of achievement. A recent refinement of the review process calls for a quarterly report on the program, followed by a site visit by the ACTION staff shortly after the end of each quarter. Consequently, any problems in the program are caught and corrected before they have time to get out of control. Program directors are kept constantly aware of their accountability, since records and files must be kept up-to-date and must be accurate and ready for inspection both quarterly and annually.

Program Implementation

The newly appointed executive director of FOCUS and the RSVP director were responsible for acquiring an office and for all details involved in establishing the program, including the hiring of additional staff. During this process, ACTION guidelines on the most desirable qualifications for the RSVP staff were available. For example, the guidelines emphasized that the secretary be a person with not only good secretarial and business skills, but also communications skills and the ability to work with both older persons and other agencies. These same general qualifications applied to all staff of the program.

During the next few months, the program staff contacted other agencies to establish volunteer stations, and recruited, oriented, and placed volunteers. Approximately twenty to forty volunteers (many of whom required transportation) were brought into the program. Next, a van was purchased and a driver hired to facilitate transportation of the volunteers to community agencies. Funds to implement this phase are usually made available during the fourth or fifth month of the first program year. In the Tuscaloosa program, the van and driver were added four months after the program began. A staff of three (which is the present number) is considered adequate for the first year, or until the volunteers number between 225 and 250, in a community with the geography and population of Tuscaloosa.

Good public relations is of primary importance in building a successful program. The public must be well informed on the program, and it is the staff's responsibility to see that proper information is disseminated as widely and as quickly as possible via all media, i.e., newspaper articles and editorials, television and radio interviews, public information announcements and feature shows, posters, church and club announcements, and speaking engagements. Information on specific assignments is gathered from the volunteer stations for use in the publicity effort. Posters are placed in areas where people of all ages gather, and the accomplishments of the volunteers are highlighted. The names of Advisory Committee members, the sponsoring agency, and the agencies that are utilizing senior volunteers are publicized in order to acquaint potential volunteers with possibilities for assignments. The advantages of the program, such as reimbursement for meals, on-the-job accident insurance, and individually developed assignments for each volunteer, are pointed out.

Use of the Media

In Tuscaloosa, the daily paper was especially cooperative at the beginning of the program. It reported the grant approval in one article, shortly thereafter featured an article on the hiring of the director, and gave important editorial support to the philosophy of the program. These three items appearing in the first months of the program emphasized that older adults had a lot to give the community and wanted to be of service, and that a program such as RSVP was designed to help them accomplish these aims. The newspaper support was useful in acquainting the community with the RSVP concept. Further publicity for the program highlighted the volunteers' activities.

The publication of human interest stories about volunteers and assignments and the submittal of regular updates of the program to all media are important in maintaining the public's awareness of RSVP. Since radio and TV stations are required by law to present public information programs, they should be utilized to disseminate information of interest to a large segment of the community.

Recruitment of Volunteers

Once the program was firmly established and older persons were actively involved in agency work throughout the community, it was possible to identify volunteers who could speak on behalf of the program. People who had the ability, interest, and motivation to talk about RSVP were extremely effective recruiters. They described how the program had affected them, and they encouraged their friends, neighbors, and relatives to become volunteers.

Newsletter articles, newspaper feature articles, radio and television, and talk shows are all excellent vehicles for volunteer expression. While the director can make arrangements for such publicity, he should step aside and let the volunteers and the agency people speak for themselves. The areas in which senior citizens congregate are good places to make recruitment speeches. By far the best means, however, after the initial impact of the program on the community is felt, is personal contact between persons involved in the program and their friends. When talking with a potential volunteer, it is helpful if a mutually known person can be named as a referral. Another successful recruiting device is the church bulletin announcement. Since many older people are regular churchgoers who read their bulletins carefully, it is well worth seeking the cooperation of ministers.

Three aspects of recruiting must be understood in undertaking this difficult job. The first is that no one method will reach all members of the target population; variety is essential. Second, repetition is absolutely required. The RSVP director must be prepared to use many approaches and return again and again to the same ones. Third, when a new option is presented, there is usually a time lag between the initial receipt of information and the response, particularly in an older and more conservative population. The use of a variety of recruitment techniques is called "shotgun recruitment" because a lot of information is given to a wide audience with the hope that it includes representatives of the target population who will respond. While it may not result in many direct recruitments, the shotgun technique should not be neglected because it channels general knowledge into the community and is essential for building local support.

In recruiting, the director may concentrate his efforts in areas where older citizens live. In the Tuscaloosa community, one of the initial recruitment moves was to contact someone who had established good rapport with older people. This individual was a Parks and Recreation Authority (PARA) coordinator who worked with senior groups both in a housing project for older adults and in several neighborhood centers. The PARA coordinator gave brief presentations on the RSVP at PARA activities. This was not a shotgun effort since the groups addressed were all older people who evidently had been participating in daytime recreational activities. The experience with such groups has been that several people frequently agree to do volunteer work immediately after the presentation. Others agree to tour agencies that need volunteers and sign up at a later time.

Followup Techniques

It is a good practice to get the names of all persons present and to inquire whether those who have no immediate interest might want to volunteer in the future. Lists of these names are kept for future reference, and phone calls and visits may be made to follow up the original contacts. Such groups should be revisited at intervals. Some potential volunteers have personal plans that prevent immediate involvement. Every effort should be made to arrange either for a delayed signup or for a return to the group.

It should always be clearly stated that the volunteer program is permanent, that assignments are available on a continuing basis, and that those volunteers who may be interested in later involvement should so indicate during the initial contact or call later. In recruiting, it is wise to use several specific examples of volunteer possibilities. It is useful to obtain as much information as possible about the potential recruits before the talk: for example, their educational level, or their interest in group or individual assignments. The agency person who issues the invitation to the RSVP director can frequently provide such information. Group volunteer recruitments can be effective and have the added advantage that the first people who join the program often recruit fellow members on an informal basis; their conversations on volunteer assignments arouse interest and help involve others.

"Be One, Reach One"

Recently, the recruitment subcommittee of the RSVP Advisory Committee (headed by a program participant) sent letters to all volunteers praising them for the work they had done and reminding them that they would like to have more volunteers. It was named the "Be One, Reach One" campaign. In this campaign, the current volunteers are asked to bring others into the program. While many people do not readily take the initiative to recruit actively, a small suggestion often stimulates activity on behalf of the program. Since one of the main purposes of the program is to involve the older citizen who is *not* active in the community, it is important to find a means of reaching that person. These "invisible" people must be located by indirect means. It has been discovered that utilization of the more active volunteers has been successful in drawing people to the program.

Rural Recruitment

Since this program is countywide, visits have been made to rural churches, stores, and neighborhood clubs. Leaders of informal groups have been contacted in an effort to get volunteers from the more sparsely populated areas. In recruiting in a rural area, it is important to recruit *groups*, since transportation is a critical factor, both in terms of time and vehicle usage. Therefore, the kind of assignments developed for and offered to volunteers must be carefully planned to accommodate the requirements of the people in those areas.

The recruitment talk must emphasize that the assignment is designed to fit the volunteer's particular needs, skills, and interests. When mentioning tasks, several should be described to show the potential volunteers that they can choose interesting assignments and do not have to be appointed to a job simply to fulfill the agency's needs. In the long run, all agency needs can be filled with the right people if care is taken in making the original assignments.

Visual Aids

Many photographs and slides of the Tuscaloosa RSVP volunteers have been taken in their assignments. A slide presentation has been prepared, and the most outstanding pictures have been enlarged for use in displays. These are valuable recruitment tools becuase they show *local* persons involved in *local* agencies serving *local* needs. The pictures used should represent a variety of volunteers doing a variety of tasks, so that the older person looking at them can identify with or visualize himself in a similar situation. Since older women out-number older men in our society and since many of the men have had fewer public service opportunities than the women, a special point should be made to attract male volunteers to make identification easier for potential volunteers.

At the onset of the program, before Tuscaloosa had developed its own visual aids, a film prepared by the national ACTION office for RSVP was used. It was very effective in illustrating the types of assignments available and the kind of people involved as volunteers. It showed that the program participants were indeed older persons, some with disabilities, working and helping other people in their community. A lightweight trifold board supplied by ACTION makes it possible to carry pictures, posters, and information sheets to meetings, fairs, and senior citizens' picnics, for use as a silent display or in conjunction with formal speeches or informal discussion. The display includes fact sheets on the local program, pictures of volunteers on their assignments, flyers, newspaper articles—anything that is eye-catching and informative—and, of course, it lists names, addresses, and phone numbers for contacting the program. Every RSVP should develop its own visual documentation of local activities as quickly as possible. There is a generally warm response to recognizable local people and scenes.

Volunteer Stations

A major factor in program implementation is the development of volunteer stations, a term designating the agencies in which volunteers serve. Developing volunteer stations is a continuing activity throughout the life of the program, beginning with the initial grant application.

Agencies that already or might utilize volunteers are approached about assigning senior volunteers. Their written response is incorporated into the grant application and is part of the initial record given to the director. It is the director's responsibility to develop a formal agreement between RSVP and the agency. The agreement is called a "Memorandum of Understanding" and includes a job description of the volunteer assignment, identification of supervisory personnel, and a clear description of the responsibilities of both the RSVP and the interested agency. The memorandum format is designed by ACTION and makes note of the Civil Rights Act as it applies to the utilization of volunteers. Responsibilities to the volunteers, such as training, transportation, and provision of meals, are outlined, and either the RSVP or the host agency takes responsibility for each item in the memorandum. The person who is directly responsible for volunteers within a given agency is listed as the supervisor, who becomes the primary contact at the agency. The memoradum is usually signed by the agency and the RSVP director. Only after the Memorandum of Understanding has been negotiated and signed can the placement of volunteers get under way.

Memoranda are updated whenever a significant staff change takes place at the agency, such as a change in the volunteer coordinator or the executive director of the agency. All the memoranda are renegotiated at the end of each year. If no major staff changes have occurred or if volunteer assignments are the same, the original agreement remains in effect. If there are changes, a new agreement may be signed.

The volunteer station specifies the number of volunteers it wishes to utilize, the times and length of service required, and the types of tasks. The RSVP director locates these personnel. The RSVP's role as a channel is evident. For example, the RSVP director locates an agency that works with young children and that needs volunteers, and he finds an older person who enjoys working with children; he then brings the two together. A time schedule agreeable to both parties, transportation, and other factors involved in the volunteer effort are then worked out on an ongoing basis.

Since the development of volunteer stations is a continuing activity, goals are set each year and are included in the renewal application. Placement agencies are classified according to types of service rendered, such as health, education, and arts instruction.

Volunteer stations are frequently developed at the request of agencies. Many times agencies will request the RSVP director's help in obtaining volunteers; the director can accept or reject such requests, depending on their suitability for older volunteers.

The number of stations utilized in a community varies greatly. Tuscaloosa has twenty-four volunteer stations. The stations also vary in the services they offer. They include, in part, a Veterans Administration Hospital, a rehabilitation center, a medical center, the American Red Cross, the Historical Preservation Society, a city board of education, Boys' Club, and nutrition program sites.

Upgrading Volunteer Placements

Agencies are requested to upgrade their volunteer placements if the volunteers prove to be responsible, creative individuals. They may ask the volunteers to undertake jobs that were not in the original description, thereby expanding opportunities. As the volunteers become familiar with agencies, they become aware of needs to be filled and are eager to be of service. Such mutual alertness is a factor in growth and job satisfaction. The director plays an active part in this process, acting as a catalyst for the growth of the ongoing stations as well as increasing the number of stations available to volunteers. As they gain responsibility and knowledge of the agency, volunteers become more sophisticated and more capable of helping the agency, and frequently they like to try more difficult assignments. New volunteers replace those who have progressed to more responsible or more interesting assignments.

Written Materials

ACTION distributes several attractive, informative pamphlets and posters on the RSVP. These are very useful to local programs, especially in the early months. The Tuscaloosa program has developed several informal mimeographed flyers with bright colors and simple designs that are handed out during recruitment efforts. These flyers reinforce the verbal and visual approaches and serve as reader references for future contacts.

One highly useful tool for keeping the program in the public eye and for providing cohesion among volunteers is a newsletter, which may be simple or as elaborate as the individual agency can manage. Developments in the program, individual achievements, and volunteer placements can be discussed in detail. The newsletter may be sent to all volunteers, volunteer stations, news media, community leaders, interested individuals and organizations, as well as governmental, political, religious, and social agencies in the area.

Recognition

One of the final stages of program implementation is recognition. Volunteers are not promoted in the strict sense of the word, and after their initial orientation, there is a tendency for them to be forgotten. Most volunteers come in, do their jobs, and leave without very much attention from the staff. While the purpose of volunteering is not to get recognition, some attention and approval are essential in maintaining the success of the volunteer program.

There are several types of recognition. First, the ACTION guidelines require that a formal recognition ceremony be held annually, just prior to the end of the program year. At this time, certificates are given to volunteers who have served for a year or longer. More recent volunteers are welcomed and recognized from the floor. Important community or state personnel deliver speeches on volunteerism and recognize the older citizens' contributions on a broad or local basis. In the Tuscaloosa community, members of the Advisory Committee structure the activity, arrange for the site, and plan the menu and program. They also secure the funding, decorate the area, help with transportation, and are responsible for details of the ceremony, with support from the RSVP staff.

The monetary support for the recognition activity comes from civic clubs outside the RSVP. One of the major men's clubs has underwritten the banquet costs of the Tuscaloosa program each year. The volunteers are not recognized for their amount of service since the *act* of service is the important factor. The regularity of their participation and the calendar length of time they have served, rather than the number of hours given, are recognized.

Informal recognition is carried out by teas held quarterly. These parties are also sponsored by groups outside the program, such as women's groups at the University of Alabama and in the community. They fund the activity, serve as hostesses, assist with transportation, and provide refreshments and decorations. In these informal activities, the volunteers' contributions are recognized on a group rather than individual level. The agency people are also recognized at the annual and the quarterly gatherings.

Most volunteers work individually or in small groups and are not aware of the full scope of the program until they attend these social gatherings. Until then, they generally have not realized that they are part of a large local, state, and national structure.

Other types of recognition include agency recognition. Many volunteers perform their assignments under agencies that also have formal recognition ceremonies. Outstanding examples are the recognition dinners at the Veterans Administration Hospital, the annual meeting of the American Red Cross, and teas held at nursing homes to recognize volunteers. Since the volunteers have an important part in these recognition functions, RSVP is often able to provide transportation.

Individual recognition of value must be a part of the RSVP function on a day-to-day basis as well. In many cases, the praise that has been given to the program by station employees is passed along to the volunteers. This may range from recognition of an outstanding job to compliments on the volunteers' dependability and empathy. One of the staff functions is to see that this praise is given as often as possible.

Conclusions

The first, and most important, conclusion is that older persons with usable skills acquired through life experiences, hobbies, and previous vocations or through their volunteer assignments can be motivated to become a vital part of their communities. Agencies that serve the community in various ways and that need extensive help in their efforts have a dependable source in the RSVP volunteers. Second, in its third year the Tuscaloosa RSVP enrolled over 255 senior volunteers, 235 of whom are currently active. These volunteers have served over 40,000 hours in twenty-four community service agencies. The cost-benefit ratio of the program is striking. The community has received these services at the astounding cumulative cost of $1.28 per hour.

More information about RSVP can be obtained by contacting ACTION in the ten federal regional offices, or by writing: ACTION, 806 Connecticut Avenue NW, Washington, D.C. 20525.

9
LOCAL VOLUNTEERISM

Jerry E. Griffin

Local service programs for the aged can benefit greatly from the proper utilization of volunteers. The goal of this brief chapter on volunteerism is to stimulate program administrators to activate or improve volunteer services and simultaneously achieve a wide range of benefits. A well-conceived volunteer program can be useful for the clients, the staff, the volunteers themselves, the local community, and those who allocate funds for such programs.

A major problem now facing most social welfare programs is that the intimate and humane connections between the taxpayer and the program beneficiary are in danger of being lost. It is not sufficient that increased appropriations are being poured into local communities for services each year, only to be spent by professionals who do the best they can to define and meet certain needs. Without general community awareness of the aging population's multiple needs and the efforts of funders to help, many programs will fail because of lack of local public support. Proper utilization of volunteers can have a far-reaching positive impact on a community's support of its senior citizens. Taxpayers need visible evidence that at least some of their taxes are being utilized for worthwhile purposes. Every taxpayer has relatives, most of whom live to retirement age and need the assistance of one or more of the services provided by tax-based programs. What social welfare service program, then, has greater potential impact on the attitudes of citizens to social welfare taxes?

Voluntary programs and services that utilize the talents of the local citizenry can give the individual taxpayer a personal rationale for the government's expenditure of his tax dollars on human services. It is not unusual to hear volunteers who are impressed with a service program remark that they are pleased that a part of their taxes is spent for such worthwhile services.

Voluntary programs also help assure the political feasibility and viability of an institution's services. They provide a direct and constant double check on what makes sense to the public. Volunteers who have direct contact with clients can be much more effective and credible than staff in interpreting client needs for sources of funds, particularly at budget request hearings held by local units of government. When an agency requests funds, it can be accused of simply wanting to protect its jobs; volunteers are exempt from such an accusation.

A few years ago, a group of informed and concerned volunteers, requesting increased appropriations for their state's mental health program, was asked to testify before the budget committee of the state legislature. The administrator of the program had prepared his formal request for an increase of less than one dollar per patient per day. This administrator was well liked by the legislature and had been in his job for over thirty years. He never requested much and always kept his institutions out of controversies. He was visibly disturbed when his volunteers presented him with factual evidence that the mental health appropriations for other states were double and triple those his own state provided. Members of the legislative budget committee were unaware that their state was so far behind the others. That state eventually made enormous increases in its mental health appropriations and is rapidly achieving a position of national leadership in the care of the mentally ill. While many factors contributed to this remarkable progress, concerned volunteers must be credited for being among the first to call attention to the state's needs. They continued to meet with the budget committee and other legislators in subsequent years to keep those needs clearly in focus.

Volunteers can provide important information about client needs to top decision-makers in probably as efficient a manner as paid administrators. The volunteer who works with a client group can go directly to a legislator, a congressman, or an elected local official. In contrast, a staff typically reports its clients' needs "up the bureaucratic ladder" wherein the information undergoes a series of successive screens and often loses its potential impact. The administrator may have better data and statistical analyses of client populations and needs, but none of these has the impact of the volunteer's information. In fact, both the administrator's formal report and the volunteer's own interpretation are needed. One without the other is likely to be less than effective.

Better program accountability and evaluation of services to the aged are of constant concern to administrators. Nevertheless, a textbook on program effectiveness is always in danger of serving logic and scientific principles more than it does the people of a local community and its citizens, to whom the program is ultimately accountable. A program may have an excellent formal system of evaluation and prove its superiority on paper, and yet have poor public relations in the local community. Utilization of volunteers can help to offset this problem as well.

Local ownership of programs is essential. No matter where the major funding originates, the program becomes viable locally only by extensively involving key interested persons within the community. The local taxpayer feels he owns nothing directly from his taxes until he can understand local matters in terms meaningful to him. Organizations that find funds and set up programs must pay as much attention to the local citizen's need in this regard as they do to the statistical reports required by funding sources.

Motivation of Volunteers

The initial motivation of a volunteer may be less important than his reasons for staying. Any service program for the aged should be so structured that it can persuade a volunteer to continue his work. The staff that recruits, trains, assigns, and supervises volunteers should be sensitive not only to initial motivations but also to new ones as they develop. For example, a volunteer may visit a nursing home as part of a musical group that performs for patients. On the first visit, he may see an elderly patient whom he knew as a child. Through subsequent visits, the volunteer may develop a special interest in his old friend and find other ways to enrich both of their lives.

A volunteer's interest may extend to a concern for the entire organization of which he is a part. He needs to be kept informed about matters that affect his work, and he should be given an opportunity to participate in organizational decision-making to the extent possible. Many factors have to be considered in helping volunteers to achieve job satisfaction. The staff that is sensitive to the value of volunteers will also be sensitive to their needs and will find numerous ways to make the volunteers' work increasingly satisfying.

Two Types of Volunteers

Two basic types of volunteers are engaged in most services for the aged. The *administrative* volunteer may hold board or committee membership positions, helping to plan, solve organizational problems, or frame policies. The *operational* volunteer supplements and extends staff functions. He is more likely to be assigned to office routines, direct client service, or fund-raising.[1] Both types of volunteers are needed, and it is not unusual for a volunteer to fill both roles, either simultaneously or at different times. Both types of volunteers may progress through a series of increasingly responsible positions. For example, the committee member may later become a committee chairman, a board member, and an officer of the board. He may hold several successively higher offices. The hierarchical structure of a social service agency is the same as that of any other agency. Factors leading to promotion include dedication, competence, friendship patterns, and actual or latent power.

The operational volunteer may move through a similar succession of tasks as the administrative volunteer, but promotional opportunities may be less appealing to the operational volunteer who enjoys his assignment. He may begin by assisting a group leader in certain activities and later assume major responsibility for the group. It is unusual, however, for the operational volunteer to accept a long-term assignment in which important program activities depend extensively upon his continued leadership. Many such volunteers are lost altogether when they are too heavily depended upon by the staff. A very real concern is their fear of being abandoned by the staff and of being faced with excessive client dependence upon them. Operational volunteers can be extremely effective if they have proper orientation and education for their work. In no case should they be regarded as amateurs, however, since much of their work may be indistinguishable from that done by professionals.

Both volunteers and staff professionals are likely to share the same motivation for human service; the volunteer is distinguished primarily by the fact that he is not paid. His unpaid status is usually known to agency clientele who, in turn, are likely to rank the volunteer's helpfulness far above that of the professional. The operational volunteers, therefore, are prized resources. Considerable attention must be given to their recruitment, orientation, and assignment and to an appropriate system of rewards.

Effective Working Relationships

Agencies sometimes encounter problems in working with both operational and administrative volunteers. While volunteers are generally regarded as essential resources, many administrators express fear of personality clashes between volunteers and staff. Aggressive volunteers may pose a threat to a staff member who fears that the volunteer is usurping his own functions. This issue may become critical with administrative volunteers who work on both policy development and its implementation. The thin line that distinguishes policy development from policy execution is often crossed by both volunteers and executives. The generally accepted principle of distinction, of course, is that boards of directors establish policy and review its effects through reports from staff. It is the administrator's responsibility to execute that policy and supervise the staff which conducts service programs in accordance with policy. The administrator also furnishes the board with information so that the board can assess the effects of its policies and make appropriate changes. A clear understanding of this principle is essential for both volunteers and staff in order to achieve workable relationships. This major point of role differentiation must be reinforced continually.

Potential problems can be largely prevented if the board gives proper care to the selection of its executive and if the executive promotes volunteers to positions of influence.

Recent social science research findings can provide guidance in the selection of people who must work together. Dr. Robert E. Bills [2] has developed a useful scheme that can be used informally to understand individuals in terms of their orientation to themselves and to others. Individuals may have a positive self-image, approaching most situations with the confidence that they will have a contribution to make. Or they may see themselves as rarely, if ever, having anything worthwhile to contribute in a working relationship with others. The positively oriented individual can be identified with a plus and the negatively oriented with a minus sign.

In addition to the plus (+) or minus (—) orientation to himself, the individual must also be understood in terms of how he typically views others. He may regard others as being capable of useful contributions equal to or superior to his own. Or he may regard others negatively, generally disregarding their abilities.

Utilizing various combinations of positive and negative orientations to self and others, four possible sets can be distinguished:

Orientation to self	Orientation to others
+	+
+	—
—	+
—	—

The individual who is oriented positively both to himself and to others (++) is obviously a valuable person whether he is an operational volunteer, committee member, chairman, board chairman, or executive. He is likely to work hard to continually validate his self-image. In addition, he is likely to incorporate the contributions of others and to give them proper credit for their efforts. Others enjoy working with him since he tends to draw out their best efforts and sets a good example through his own work.

The individual who is oriented positively to himself but negatively toward others (+—) may, in fact, be extremely capable in his own right. At the same time, he tends to dominate others and finds many ways to achieve his own ends. He may make a fetish of his own leadership abilities, convincing the less aggressive that he is the best choice for leadership positions. He tends to talk longer and louder in meetings and wins more decisions than he loses. All too frequently, such persons are found in high positions of leadership. They can virtually "lead others around by the nose." Casual observation of their performance in voluntary organizations may show that they are doing a good job. A more careful study of their achievement, however, often produces a different picture. For example, individuals in a group who may have initially joined with a ++ orientation are pushed toward a —+ orientation. Their self-confidence is eroded in the presence of a dominant +— person. Their effectiveness may be reduced to a minimum, and they may eventually leave the organization. If they do not leave, their adjustment to the situation is likely to take the form of "rubber stamping" the wishes of the leader. In either case, the results are subtle and gradual. The organization's overall effectiveness is gradually eroded.

Individuals who have a negative orientation toward themselves but a positive one toward others (—+) are easily led by almost anyone who is willing to lead. Under the leadership of a ++ person, they can develop their own capabilities and self-confidence. The leader with a +— orientation, however, may severely reduce their effectiveness.

Those who tend to see both themselves and others in a negative light (——) are usually cynical. They are generally dissatisfied with many things, as if to say, "I know I don't have the answer, but buddy you don't either!"

Several immediate implications can be drawn from this discussion. The practitioner who finds this scheme to be useful will continue to see additional applications. For example, the agency executive and *all* of his program managers should be ++ people. They will bring the best performance out of each other and will help their program staff to be productive. It is also wise to select ++ volunteers for key supervisory roles. They will bring out the best in others. The —+ and +— volunteers can be distributed among various activities where they will be shielded or provided with proper controls, as appropriate. A bright, aggressive +— person will need to be watched carefully to prevent his taking over a succession of activities where he is likely to cause difficulty. These same principles and concepts may be applied to the formation of task groups, whether comprised of volunteers or staff. The selection of task group leaders is critical; if all members of a group are expected to contribute to the group's efforts, the leader must have a ++ orientation. If a person has a strong +— orientation, he should be given a job to do all by himself. He may do the job well and may appreciate the fact that he did it alone.

Starting Volunteer Services

Services to the aged have developed so rapidly in recent years that many administrators may not have devoted sufficient time to getting volunteer services started. With increasing program stability and more secure funding channels, more time and opportunities are available to recruit and utilize volunteers.

First, the administrator and his staff need to examine their service programs carefully to find places where the operational volunteer can be utilized. While this is being done, a member of the staff should be selected to head up the developing volunteer program. Above all, the person selected should be interested in the new job and should be enthusiastic in his contacts with others. He will develop job descriptions, and recruit and orient operational volunteers.

The coordinator of volunteers may be able to benefit from the counsel and assistance of others in the community who have extensive experience with volunteers. Many cities have a volunteer service bureau that can provide assistance. If there is no established community program, institutions in the local community that have utilized volunteers can offer advice. For example, hospitals, schools, and churches use volunteers regularly, and their experiences can aid a new coordinator of voluntary services to the aged.

Once a reliable consultant has been located, it is helpful to bring the consultant to the agency to look over all service programs for the aged and to help identify the jobs which volunteers could perform. The experienced coordinator of volunteers will usually find many more jobs for volunteers than the agency staff can.

Volunteer jobs should be described, and the skills needed should be identified. This information forms the basis for recruiting activities. Before recruitment begins, however, other preparations should be made so that newly recruited volunteers can be trained and assigned soon after they become available.

There are numerous sources of volunteers: college students, civic organizations, social and study clubs, churches, and agencies of all kinds. As the coordinator of volunteers makes the agency's needs known through the mass media, brochures, and speeches to groups, he should not forget that the most effective method of recruitment is the one-to-one individualized approach.[3] Although publicity is essential in locating potentially interested persons, personal contacts are more crucial to recruitment.

Maintaining good records as a reference for contacting volunteers is extremely important. Records are also needed to keep track of volunteer's service so that awards may be given properly.

The administrative volunteer is familiar to every agency that has a board of directors. Too often, however, insufficient time and attention are given to this volunteer between board meetings. By merely attending a monthly board meeting, most board members cannot develop enough familiarity with the agency's operations to be effective policy-makers. The administrative volunteer should be utilized in a variety of ways both to assist the agency and to develop his own knowledge and skills.

One major way the administrative volunteer can be utilized is through the establishment of program advisory units that parallel the agency's internal staff organization. Among other duties, the advisory groups can make a continuing study of program operations and suggestions to the board for improvements. Hence, each service program can benefit from an advisory group.

Administrative volunteers can also be used to conduct periodic needs surveys. With the assistance of competent staff, volunteers can approach other organizations and individuals in the community with a set of interview questions concerning the needs of the aged or certain aspects of the organization they represent. Such surveys provide valuable feedback data for the board of directors and administrator. In addition, they enable key community persons who may know little about the agency to have personal briefings.

An organized and well-developed effort can result in a host of volunteers doing a great variety of tasks both within and on behalf of an agency serving the aged in a community. The enormous public relations value of all such efforts combined is not inconsiderable. Thus it is that the utilization of volunteers should be begun on a serious basis. Anything less than careful preparation and continuing attention not only will result in the failure of the volunteer program, but also will produce negative relationships within the community.

Volunteer services have been a secondary consideration too long. They need the first-rate attention of administrators and agency boards. The rewards can be extensive—for the elderly, the agency as a whole, and the volunteers as well.

Notes

1. Harriet H. Naylor, *Volunteers Today—Finding, Training, and Working with Them* (New York: Association Press, 1967), p. 25.

2. Robert E. Bills, *A System of Assessing Affectivity* (Tuscaloosa: University of Alabama Press, 1975); and Robert E. Bills, *About People and Teaching*, Bureau of School Service, University of Kentucky, December 1955, Vol. 28-#2.

3. Ruth E. Ward, *Volunteer Leadership Recruitment in Selected Character Building Organizations*, Ed.D. dissertation, Teachers' College, Columbia University, 1963.

10
THE ROLE OF VOLUNTEERISM

N. Philip Grote

In 1974, a survey conducted by the U.S. Census Bureau and sponsored by ACTION revealed that one out of every four Americans over the age of thirteen does some form of volunteer work.[1] Of the population sampled, 20 percent were aged fifty-five and over. That is, one out of every five Americans aged fifty-five and over were doing volunteer work. Of this group, the majority devoted twenty-five to ninety-nine hours a year, and approximately 10 percent provided at least 300 hours of voluntary service per year. Overall, it appears that the fifty-five and over age group is giving a great deal of its time to various types of volunteer work. What does this statement mean? What are older people getting from these activities? What types of activities are older people involved in?

In answer to the first question, some direct inferences can be made. The first inference relates to the life span of our citizenry. As a developed country, a larger percentage of the U.S. population is in the ranks of the elderly than is true in most of the developing countries. This has immediate consequences for the elderly's utilization of leisure time. Although 5 percent of the older population is institutionalized, the overwhelming majority is not and they remain fairly active. Many of these older people are retired and now have fewer family obligations. They are "freed" from other work-related activities so that theoretically they can pursue the things they were always interested in but never had the time to do earlier in life. Often, however, they have more time on their hands in retirement than they had really anticipated. This segment presents a unique opportunity for recruitment. Here are people who are interested in being involved with others, desire to contribute to the community's well-being, and often have skills or resources that can be utilized for the benefit of others. Finding the right person to perform a specific task or service might be a problem, but it can usually be accomplished when the coordinator of volunteers is trained in the use of volunteers and when a creative individual desires volunteer services in an agency.

The second question, "What are older people getting from these activities?," is interesting from several perspectives. This question involves the functions of volunteerism in American society. One of its first functions is directly related to the individual who performs the voluntary act or activity. This function is the personal satisfaction that comes from aiding another human being or performing a beneficial service. Too often the elderly (justifiably) begin to feel rejected by society or, in turn, to reject society. The effective engagement of older persons in voluntary activities often helps them overcome their feelings of uselessness, isolation, and alienation, and gives them a productive role. This function is generally accomplished through the consummatory/self-expressive-oriented volunteer, as well as the philanthropic and service-oriented volunteers. (These types of volunteers will be discussed in a later section.)

Another function of volunteerism relates to the changing role of the elderly in our pluralistic society. Besides the function of direct satisfaction of needs, particularly the social or associational needs of the elderly—the need to be around others—there is an important role they play in the political processes in our society. As the population grows and the percentage of elderly in the population increases, their needs and their position in the society will require greater public awareness. The elderly have articulate spokesmen for their position within their own ranks.

With regard to the third question, "What types of activities are older people involved in?," see Appendix A which lists areas of volunteer work and activities. This listing is not intended to be exhaustive but rather to stimulate those working with volunteers to use the list creatively. The fact that one area lists specific types of activities does not mean that volunteers in that area should be limited to those activities; hence the separation of areas and activities.

Arnold Rose discusses three functions of voluntary associations in American democracy.[2] Although he speaks of these as general functions, they may be extrapolated to apply to older persons. The first function Rose mentions is to "distribute power over social life among a very large proportion of the citizenry, instead of allowing it to be concentrated in the elected representatives above." This change is being effected by the emergence of issue-oriented groups like the National Caucus of the Black Aged and the Gray Panthers.

Rose's second function is to provide "a sense of satisfaction with modern democratic processes because they help the ordinary citizen to see how the processes function in limited circumstances, of direct interest to himself." This is an important role for volunteers, particularly the elderly. They contribute to legislative or economic processes that directly influence their well-being through local, national, or international organizations oriented to monitoring or introducing legislation. Examples of such organizations are the International Senior Citizens Association, National Council on the Aging, and National Retired Teachers Association-American Association of Retired Persons

(NRTA-AARP). The process of developing this type of economic/legislative activity can be a difficult and frustrating process unless the groups (especially the elderly who have rarely experienced social action) directly perceive the issues and interests.

The third function that Rose discusses is related to providing "a social mechanism for continually instituting social change." The change function becomes critical with the elderly for several reasons. First, as mentioned above, an issue must be felt or perceived directly before mobilization for change can take place. Once formed, the mechanism can rapidly become inactive unless there are long-term goals and issues to be dealt with and to perpetuate the action group. Some of these issues are discussed briefly in a later section of this chapter.

Definition of Volunteerism

When discussing volunteers, the question arises "What is a volunteer?" Basically, the term connotes an individual who performs, without coercion, a necessary activity for an organization, group, or individual and who does not receive financial remuneration for the task performed. In addition, a group of individuals can give volunteer services jointly. The rewards are generally psychological or social, and the activities performed are motivated by personal preference.

A more conventional definition of volunteers is as follows:

> Volunteers have three typical functions—giving direct service, fund raising, and policy determination. The greatest number are involved in providing services, from being Big Brothers to providing casework services that would be professional if the volunteer received pay. Fund raising activities range from ringing doorbells to writing copy for brochures and making spot announcements on television. Policy determination is the role of board members at local, regional, or national levels. [3]

The description of volunteers as "free help" should be avoided. Too often, this description has a stigmatizing effect, devaluing those who give their services, presenting problems for those to whom the services are given, and harming working relationships with coordinators, administrators, and volunteers. Elderly volunteers who rightfully tend to value their past experience as an asset to those for whom they volunteer their services are particularly harmed.

Sources of Volunteers

The question of where to find volunteers has confronted many coordinators and managers, not only when their programs are initiated but also once their activities are ongoing. A basic answer to the problem lies in getting to know the community—not just key governmental personnel but all organizations, associations, and groups, locally, statewide, and nationally. Volunteers are frequently thought of as neat little bands of middle-class clubs or organizations that are carrying out their "theme of the month." While this perspective may have had some validity once, it probably does not today.

Volunteers can be recruited from everywhere. Every community has many social groupings interested in potential placements for volunteers. They can provide volunteers through their own programs or recruit them from other personal contacts. Businesses often are interested in providing volunteers. They may "lend out" executives or technical personnel for a limited amount of time to work on community projects. They may want older volunteers to talk about the benefits and problems of retirement in their preretirement employee training programs. Civic clubs or associations frequently supply their members on a volunteeer basis for activities such as beautification programs, social service programs, or door-to-door campaigns to stimulate action on various issues. Churches often provide personnel for community projects; frequently, they also make their facilities available for meetings and furnish transportation for volunteers. Other community-based resources are the small neighborhood self-help associations, minority programs, and other community groups that are not quite so visible. The coordinator of volunteer programs has to go to these locations to seek out these groups. Through a creative imagination and some footwork and telephoning, the coordinator can establish a reserve of volunteers for almost any activity. Only action can bring action.

Voluntary Versus Bureaucratic Structures

As illustrated above, the majority of volunteers can be found in what voluntary action scholars have called the voluntary association, voluntary organization, or voluntary action group. Most such associations are locally based, formal or informal clusterings of members with specialized interests who have made a deliberate choice for membership and who may resign at any time.[4] They may be professional associations such as the NRTA-AARP, the Lady Garment Workers' Union, or the American Association of Planners, or they may be civic groups such as the Elks and Lions Clubs. A voluntary organization becomes a more specialized form of social organization when its primary focus is on the coordination, training, and placement of volunteers within a suitable setting. The structure and processes of this kind of organization are very similar to those of the classic bureaucratic model familiar to us in everyday life. One of the basic differences between the voluntary organization and bureaucratic structures in our society lies in the voluntary organization's humanitarian approach and involvement with people as opposed to goods. A *service*, not a *product*, is being delivered.

Classification of Volunteers

Knowledge of the various types of volunteers available can be a useful tool in the direct selection of a volunteer for an agency. The proposed classification covers all age groups and all social classes. As mentioned earlier, not everyone perceives the role of volunteer in the same way, and many persons who volunteer do not always see themselves as "volunteers." In this regard, the typology presented by David Smith is of interest. Smith defines the volunteer and describes the major types of voluntary action.[5]

The first type Smith lists is the *philanthropic/funding-oriented volunteer*. This is the person that everyone views as the "money giver," but this perception is only partially true. This type also inclues those who are primarily interested in raising or distributing funds for nonprofit and voluntary organizations to further philanthropic efforts in the areas of health, religion, welfare, the environment, education, or other special causes. Such a volunteer is probably concerned more with the economics of survival and the maintenance of the voluntary organization than with direct service.

Smith's second, third, fourth, and fifth types of volunteers are more performance oriented. They are the *service oriented, issue/cause oriented, consummatory/self-expressive oriented*, and the *occupational/economic self-interest oriented*. Before discussing these types, a caveat is in order. These types are ideal models of the functions they perform, but in reality each overlaps the other. None exists in a pure form. While one type may be focused on, the actions and functions of other types are incorporated in that single type.

The *service-oriented* type of volunteer—the Red Cross, hospital, or court volunteer—is the most traditional type. The primary function of this volunteer is to provide direct service to others. With specific regard to older volunteers in this category, they usually perform services such as friendly visitor, telephone reassurance, or transportation. As both Naylor[6] and Smith[7] point out, there appears to be a trend in volunteerism away from the concept of "doing for" toward that of "doing with" and "doing by" the groups/individuals involved. This leads to other types of volunteerism that are more and more attacking the roots of problems rather than the symptoms.[8]

Issue/cause-oriented volunteers are individuals or groups that gravitate to public issues. The issues may be broad or narrow, national or local, humanitarian or material. Groups of elderly volunteers or groups working with the elderly provide some excellent examples of this type. One example, the Gray Panthers, is a national movement designed to bring the youth and elderly together in order to improve the status of both groups. By 1974, this organization had local chapters in thirteen states.[9] Another group in this classification is the National Caucus of the Black Aged, an organization concerned with determining and correcting conditions that adversely affect the black elderly.[10] Many other groups exist on the international, national, and local levels that are action oriented to change attitudes, conditions, or the general welfare of older people. Some fall into other major categories; a few will be discussed below, and the others are listed at the end of this chapter (see Appendix B).

The fourth type of volunteers that Smith discusses is the *consummatory/ self-expressive* type. This is possibly one of the most valued forms of volunteerism for the elderly themselves, but one of the least valued and most widely ignored by others. This type enjoys activities for their own sake and for the sake of self-expression and self-realization. Recent literature focusing on the social aspects of aging indicates that the consummatory/self-expressive type of volunteer may be one of the most important aspects of volunteerism for the elderly. It brings into focus the whole realm of life-satisfaction, longevity, health, and socialization for the elderly of the United States. [11]

In a discussion with Harriet Naylor in 1974 concerning volunteerism among the elderly, she pointed out that the elderly need an arena for self-expressive activities, and that arena is quite possibly volunteer associations and organizations. Older persons in American society have too long been cast off much as potentially recycled hard goods. With the advent of "Golden Age" clubs and senior citizens' groups at the local level, an attempt to work with and for the elderly has begun. [12] Through these groups, the elderly are striving for renewed self-esteem, greater satisfaction with life, and fuller self-realization. Many older people have worked very hard to achieve a "good" retirement—supposedly one of the benefits of our society—but upon reaching that state have realized that it is not the "leisure life" they had envisioned. One of the most important revelations is that they miss the pleasure of old associates and friends. Naylor speculates that this social-psychological impact may account for the high mortality rate among newly retired persons. Although volunteer outlets are available, more voluntary associations serving an integrative function for social life need to be made available. If these associations come into being, it is quite possible that the mortality rate for newly retired persons might decline significantly. Rose maintains that this socializing experience is one of the main functions which voluntary associations or organizations serve in our society. [13]

The last type of volunteerism, *occupational/economic self-interest oriented*, is not generally viewed as a voluntary activity. It is primarily concerned with furthering the economic or occupational interests of its participants. These activities may be seen in business groups, professional associations, trade unions, and other groups working to improve the conditions or quality of life for its members. Participants do not receive profits from the group to which they belong; instead, they receive long-term benefits from their paid membership in the organization. Benefits may range from lower insurance rates, higher fringe benefits, information services, or services of other types. With older people, this type of volunteerism is reflected in various senior citizens' groups such as NRTA-AARP, the Retired Railroad Workers Association, or the Retired Officers Association. Some organizations may deal with special benefits to which members are entitled, including life or burial insurance, discount rates on planes or buses for vacations and travel, specialized updates on new activities in former occupations, information on food purchases, health and medical services, and retirement homes or centers. This type of volunteerism was originally related to the establishment of trade unions which were later in the forefront of service- and issue-oriented activities designed to improve poor working conditions, raise income levels, and enhance the quality of life for the laborer. [14] Today, this ethic has taken various organizational forms and is being integrated into the retirement and preretirement plans of various occupational and professional groups.

In summary, this chapter reviews some basic questions relating to the number of elderly in active volunteer programs, the activities they are involved in, and what they are personally obtaining from their involvement. The question of who is a volunteer, along with some of the functions of volunteerism, are discussed. Both suggest that the public, as well as those who coordinate and administer volunteer programs, have only a limited perception of volunteerism. In an attempt to broaden this perception, older people are being looked at as sources of volunteers, and efforts are being made to fit the volunteer into various organizational structures. The typology of voluntary action offered here shows how older volunteers might be linked with various sectors of the society so that they might find a personally satisfying experience, maintain an integrative feeling, and develop a sense of personal worth.

APPENDIX A

ORGANIZATIONS THAT DEAL WITH VOLUNTEERS

Listed below are some of the national associations or organizations, both private and governmental, that deal with volunteerism. Many of the organizations listed specifically provide supporting information and resources for the elderly. Others are primarily involved in training and education, information and referral, contracts and grants, or research and analysis dealing with general volunteerism or services for the elderly. Contact with these organizations may provide the practitioner with some useful materials to aid program development or may suggest new ways of dealing with old problems.

The *Green Sheets* of the National Center for Voluntary Action (NCVA) has been a key resource for developing this listing. NCVA also collects information on ongoing projects and serves as a clearinghouse for information related to all areas of volunteerism.

As mentioned earlier, this listing is not exhaustive. Those interested in finding additional organizations or resources for the elderly can make inquiries through the organizations listed here.

International Senior Citizens Association, Inc.
11753 Wilshire Boulevard
Los Angeles, Calif. 90025

International Federation on Aging
1909 K Street NW
Washington, D.C. 20006

The Alliance on Voluntarism
1221 University Avenue
Boulder, Colo. 80302

Administration on Aging
Social and Rehabilitation Services
U.S. Department of Health, Education, and Welfare
HEW South Building, Room 3086
330 C Street SW
Washington, D.C. 20201

Special Committee on Aging
United States Senate
G-233 Senate Office Building
Washington, D.C. 20510

Older American Volunteer Programs
ACTION
806 Connecticut Avenue NW
Washington, D.C. 20036

Food and Nutrition Services
U.S. Department of Agriculture
Washington, D.C. 20250

National Council of Senior Citizens
1511 K Street NW
Washington, D.C. 20005

U.S. Department of Housing and Urban Development
Senior Program Officer
Room 10136
Washington, D.C. 20410

American Association of Retired Persons
National Retired Teachers Association
1909 K Street NW
Washington, D.C. 20006

The Gray Panthers
3700 Chestnut Street
Philadelphia, Pa. 19104

National Caucus of the Black Aged
4400 West Girard Avenue
Philadelphia, Pa. 19104

National Association of Retired Federal Employees
1533 New Hampshire Avenue NW
Washington, D.C. 20036

Office of Public Affairs
Urban Mass Transportation Administration

U.S. Department of Transportation, Room 9330
Washington, D.C. 20590

Gerontological Society
One Dupont Circle, Suite 520
Washington, D.C. 20036

National Interfaith Coalition on Aging
220 South Hull Street
Athens, Ga. 30601

National Center for Voluntary Action
1785 Massachusetts Avenue NW
Washington, D.C. 20036

National Information Center on Voluntarism, Inc.
1221 University Avenue
Boulder, Colo. 80302

APPENDIX B

AREA OF SERVICE AND
SERVICE TASKS THAT
CAN BE PERFORMED
BY OLDER VOLUNTEERS

The following, a partial listing of types of volunteerism, areas of voluntary services, and service roles for elderly volunteers, should be viewed as ways older volunteers may be utilized. A key to placement of the volunteer is meeting organization or agency needs with the volunteers' needs, not haphazard placement.

I. Types of Volunteerism

A. Service Oriented

B. Issue/Cause Oriented

C. Consummatory/Self-Expressive Oriented

D. Occupational/Economic Self-Interest Oriented

E. Philanthropic/Funding Oriented

II. Areas of Voluntary Services

ACTION Programs
Adult Education
Air Pollution

Beautification Programs
Boards
Business/Industry Involvement
Campaign and Political Projects
City and County Governments
Civic Affairs
Civic Organizations
Civil Rights
Communications and Public Relations
Community Agencies or Organizations
Consumer Services
Counseling and Guidance Assistance
Courts and Probation
Crisis Centers
Cultural Enrichment
Day Care/Head Start
Disaster Relief Programs
Drug Abuse/Alcoholism
Employment
Energy
Entrepreneurship
Executive Assistance
Family-Youth and Children-Oriented Services
Federal Surplus Property Disposal
Food Programs
Funding, Fund-Raising, and Related Resources
Green-Thumb Program
Handicapped: Physical/Mental
Health
Hospitals
Housing/Home Repairs and Maintenance
Information and Referral
Intercultural/Disadvantaged Assistance
Interracial/Interethnic/Interreligious, and other Intergroup
    Relations
Leadership Development
Learning Disabilities
Legal Assistance
Legal Rights: Law Enforcement and Crime Prevention
Library Assistance
Mental Health, General
Mental Health, Retarded
Newspapers/Newsletters
Noise Control

Nursing Homes
Nutrition Education
Parks, Land, and Endangered Species
Physical Environment/Conservation and Action Programs
Planned Parenthood
Planning or Development Agencies
Population Control
Poverty Program Assistance
Prisons and Juvenile Institutions
Reading Assistance
Recreation
Recycling Programs
Religious and Church Activities
Research and Resource Assistance
Retirement and Preretirement Program Assistance
Schools
Secretarial and Clerical Assistance
Solid Waste
Technical Assistance
Transportation
Tutoring
Venereal Diseases
Veterans Administration Organizations
Vocational Action Centers or Bureaus
Water Pollution
Welfare Assistance
Youth Services/Delinquency Prevention

III. Service Roles for Older Volunteers

Activities of Day Center Facilities for Elderly, for Children
Administrative Assistance
Aid to Farmers
Aides in Geriatric Wards or State Hospitals
Aiding in Red Cross Safety Programs
Aiding Unwed Mothers
Assistance in Information Collection of Senior Citizens' Centers
    and Clubs
Assistance in Interviewing for Food Assistance Programs
Assistance in Outreach Programs to Find People in Need
Assistance in Physical or Occupational Therapy Programs
Big Brother or Big Sister Programs/Foster Grandparents/
    Guardianship
Bookkeeping Assistance/Clerical Tasks

Canvassing for Voters/for Candidates

Carpentry/Plumbing/Electrical Home Repairs and Maintenance

Committee Work on Community Programs (Governmental and Nongovernmental)

Community Activities (Picnics, Parties, Educational Programs)

Community Planning Agency Assistance

Developing Playgrounds and Parks

Emergency Room or Hospital Aide

Flea Market Operations

Friendly Visitor

Health Education Group Assistance (Heart and Lung Association, Diabetes, etc.)

Housework Assistance Aide

Housing Authority Assistance

Legal Services Assistance

Library Assistance

Lobbying and Advocacy Activities

Meal Sites/Multipurpose Center/Meals-on-Wheels

Medical Assistance Services

Musical Activities (Teaching Instruments, Directing Choirs, etc.)

Nursing Home Activities

Organization and Implementation of Beautification Programs: Refurbishment of Parks and Recreation Areas; Cleanup Work in Cities and/or Rural Areas

Organization/Assistance with ASPCA

Outreach Worker Assistance

Placement, Maintenance, and Selection of Volunteers

Placement, Training, Recruitment, and Screening of Senior Volunteers for Local Voluntary Action Center or Bureau

Police-Community Relations

Preparation of Data for Data Processing

Preretirement Counseling

Probation/Parole Programs

Production of Arts or Crafts for Program Support

Providing Transportation/Driving Community Service Vehicles

Raising Money for Needy

Recycling Center Services

Senior Citizen Volunteer Advisory Councils (Planning)

Social Security Aides

Sponsoring Art Centers

Suicide Prevention Center Services

Supplement and Reinforce the Subprofessional Roles

Teacher's Aide

Teaching Art

Teaching Babysitting Skills to Teenagers

Teaching Employment Skills/Budgeting/Buying, etc.

Teaching Home Management Skills

Teaching Skills, Crafts, or Arts to Scouts

Technical and Financial Advice to Struggling Businesses

Telephone Answering for Information and Referral Systems

Telephone Reassurance Checks/Hot Line/Information and
    Referral Services

Tour Guides for Historical/Art/Public Places

Tutoring

Working in Church Activities

Working in Thirft Stores

Working with Aged, Handicapped, or Emotionally Disturbed

Working with Disaster Relief Programs (Providing Food,
    Clothing, Household Equipment)

Working with Foster Children

Working with Hospitals and Clinics

Working with Placement Services/Career Counseling

Notes

1. ACTION, *American Volunteer: 1974* (Washington, D.C.: U.S. Government Printing Office, 1974).

2. Arnold Rose, "A Theory of the Functions of Voluntary Organizations in Contemporary Social Structure." In *Theory and Method in the Social Sciences* (Minneapolis: University of Minnesota Press, 1954), p. 51.

3. Richard J. Anderson, "Volunteers and Paraprofessionals." In *Contemporary Social Work: An Introduction to Social Work and Social Welfare*, edited by Ronald Brieland, Lela B. Costin, and Charles R. Atherton (New York: McGraw-Hill Book Co., 1975), p. 380.

4. George A. Theodorson and Achilles G. Theodorson, *A Modern Dictionary of Sociology* (New York: Thomas Y. Crowell Co., 1969).

5. David H. Smith, *Research and Communication Needs in Voluntary Action.* Occasional Paper No. 2. (Washington, D.C.: Center for a Voluntary Society, 1972).

6. Harriet Naylor, "Voluntarism with and by the Elderly." In *Foundations of Practical Gerontology*, edited by Rosamonde Boyd and Charles G. Oakes, 2d ed. (Columbia, S.C.: University of South Carolina Press, 1973).

7. Smith, op. cit.

8. Ibid.

9. Harriet L. Kipps, *Clearinghouse Green Sheets* (Washington, D.C.: National Center for Voluntary Action, 1974), p. 264.

10. Ibid.

11. Robert J. Atchley, *The Social Forces in Later Life: An Introduction to Social Gerontology* (Belmont, Calif.: Wadsworth Publishing Co., 1972); David Dye, Mortimer Goodman, Melvin Roth, Nina Bley, and Kathryn Jensen, "The Older Adult Volunteer Compared to the Non-Volunteer," *The Gerontologist* (Summer 1973): 215-218; and Naylor, op. cit.

12. Naylor, op. cit., p. 195.

13. Rose, op. cit.

14. Smith, op. cit.

PART IV
Advocacy and Ombudsman Programs

11
CONSUMER ADVOCACY

Solomon G. Jacobson

In late 1968, Mel Ravitz, the president of Detroit's Common Council, was receiving numerous complaints about nursing homes, and he felt he needed assistance in dealing with them. He consulted with the officials of the local Department of Public Health but found that their ability to respond beyond their legal mandate was limited. A health department official suggested that a citizens' body be organized to serve as a consumer advocacy group. Since there were no models for such an organization, Ravitz assigned the organizational task to Charles Chomet who was then working on a social work field placement with the Detroit Common Council. Chomet had previously been director of a poverty program in Illinois and had returned to Michigan to get his Master's degree in social work, and so he had some knowledge of the advocacy procedures.

In June 1969, Ravitz offered a solution to the Detroit Common Council to establish a public interest group to maintain high-quality care where it existed and to encourage such care where it did not exist. The resolution passed. The first organizational meeting of the advocacy group was sponsored by the City of Detroit Department of Public Health, with the understanding that the department would remove itself from the role of sponsor once the citizens' organization was formed. The first meeting was well attended by representatives from unions, civic associations, universities, and retired persons. This group was in unanimous agreement that such an advocacy group was needed. A series of organizational meetings were arranged with Chomet as the temporary chairman.

Overview

In 1969, the situation relating to nursing homes in Detroit was similar to that in many other areas of the country. There was a very aggressive and active association of nursing home proprietors who had extensive working relationships with state legislators. The licensing of nursing homes in Michigan was the responsibility of the State Department of Public Health. In some cases, as in Detroit, the state department delegated the licensing function to the local department, which also made inspections and recommended actions to the state agency. The regulations used by the delegated regulatory agencies were often stricter than those required by the state department. In Detroit, the working relationship between the state and the city public health agencies was very uneasy.

The local inspectors were stricter than the state, and several times recommended closing a home that the state had allowed to remain open. The Detroit inspectors found that a number of homes were in substantial violation of basic regulations. Specifically, the homes had staff shortages (especially nurses' aides) and improper sanitation practices, with the result that many patients were developing bedsores. Constant disputes arose between the nursing home operators and the city health inspectors. These disputes formed the basis for the later intervention of the state nursing home associations which resulted in the state frequently overriding local recommendations. There were constant arguments over lines of authority. To add to the general confusion, a number of newspaper articles on nursing home conditions appeared and were usually answered by press releases from the nursing home associations accusing the local Department of Public Health of attempting to damage the industry.

Nursing home rules and regulatory processes in Michigan were somewhat more comprehensive than those nationally, and homes with the most obvious violations had been closed down. Even so, there were still numerous complaints and many substandard homes in operation when Chomet began chairing the organizational meetings of the proposed advocacy group.

Membership of the Advocacy Group

The original citizens' organizing group met frequently during the summer and fall of 1969. It was decided that the organization would attempt to represent the interests of nursing home patients, but would probably have few, if any, representatives from active patients. It was also deemed unwise to draw any substantial numbers from persons who had parents or other relatives in nursing homes. The rationale was that both patients and relatives might fear retaliatory action such as eviction by the nursing home. The greatest support came from retired workers and young professionals. The retired workers were largely associated with the United Automobile Workers, many of whom had been active in organizing that powerful union. They were personally acquainted with conditions in nursing homes through visits to friends and relatives. They had been angered by the conditions they discovered and by the apparent lack of concern exhibited by some nursing home operators. The professionals felt that the recent introduction of federal financing into nursing homes through Medicaid and Medicare made it imperative that there be independent watchdog associations to assure that federal dollars did not go to support substandard facilities. The institutional affiliations and backing of the professionals and retired persons in the early discussions provided a strong basis for organizing a consumer advocacy group.

The decision was made to extend the interest of the group to homes for the aged and after-care facilities such as boarding homes and permit homes. The organizing group agreed that, although they were concerned with patients of all ages in such facilities, they would first concentrate on the conditions of elderly patients in nursing homes. Initially, the most extensive discussion centered on the admission of nursing home operators or their representatives to the advocacy organization. The retired union workers argued strongly against this move. They advocated an independent consumer organization with no ties to the industry, reasoning that it would take a considerable amount of time for consumers to understand the complications of the nursing home business. They felt that the industry made exaggerated claims and would distract, rather than educate, the membership. As a result, they maintained, the group could easily spend two or three years in debate and discussion with proprietary home owners instead of taking direct action. The union workers' viewpoint prevailed, and it was decided that any person owning or employed by a nursing home or similar facility would be excluded from membership. In the fall of 1969, the Citizens for Better Care (CBC) in Nursing Homes, Homes for the Aged, and Other After-Care Facilities was officially established.

Selection of Advocacy Issues

CBC's first year was largely spent in writing the bylaws and finding a permanent location for the organization. The initial funding came from membership dues which paid for stationery and stamps. The affiliation with the City of Detroit Department of Public Health was officially terminated, and the CBC elected Chomet as their first president. Chomet encouraged the members to select as initial areas of investigation issues that could make an important impact on the nursing home situation. The CBC formed an executive board that would have policy-making powers and would establish working committees for preparing the preliminary background on the issues.

The criteria for selecting issues were suggested by Chomet and have remained as guides for the organization. Namely, an issue must be important to the membership; it must be clearly focused; there must be a reasonable chance that it will be successfully addressed; and there must be sufficient personnel and resources available to carry out the activities in resolving the problem.

The criteria for selecting issues were applied to all CBC activities. The following illustration from CBC's early history demonstrates their effectiveness as standard operating criteria for advocacy groups. In its effort to examine and follow up on complaints against nursing homes, CBC discovered that the State

Department of Public Health refused to disclose its inspection records to any person or group. However, the city of Detroit, as the delegated inspection agency, opened its records for review. After familiarizing themselves with the content of the city's records, CBC requested permission to review the state records in Lansing. Access was denied. This refusal became the focus for discussion and debate among the membership.

The first action taken was to request permission to examine the results of nursing home inspections maintained by the Department of Public Health in the state capital. This request was formally denied by a letter from the department's director. He indicated that the Administrative Procedures Act stated that information collected by a public agency on a private business was confidential and could not be released. CBC argued the information should be public record since public funds accounted for nearly 70 percent of nursing home revenues in the state. This argument proved ineffective, as did appeals to state legislators and the editorial support of some newspapers. The CBC leadership agreed that gaining access to inspection records would be a major issue: it was important; it was clear; it could be successfully attempted; and there were sufficient personnel and resources available to do followup.

Strategy

The next major decision was to formulate a strategy for impelling the state director of public health to open the records of nursing home inspections to the newly formed advocacy group. Since formal requests and political pressure had proved ineffective, the only recourse appeared to be the courts. Chomet contacted several lawyers and found several young advocates who were interested in the case. They researched the issue and decided that a law suit was the most effective approach. They argued that the records should be made public since federal and state tax dollars were being used to finance a large portion of nursing home operations. The state countered that the records of inspections related to the business operation of private concerns and, therefore, should not be made public. In addition, some state officials expressed concern that CBC would use the records to harass nursing home operators. The State Department of Public Health was committed to its role of consultant to nursing home operators and frequently resented the intrusion of the advocacy group. The nursing home operators and their associations were naturally concerned, but at this time they were involved in a bitter argument with the state over reimbursement rates and found the disclosure of records to be a minor issue.

In 1971, the law suit was filed in the lower state circuit court and received considerable publicity. The state prepared for a defense of its position, realizing that loss of the case could result in the forced disclosure of many types of records covered by the Administrative Procedures Act. In some ways, the state officials welcomed the suit on the basis that it would clarify certain issues. They exhibited no overt hostility to CBC for its action. The case took many months to come before the court, but it was successful. The state appealed and CBC was once again successful. Nearly three years later, in the spring of 1974, the State Supreme Court ruled that the State Department of Public Health must make reports of nursing home inspections available to the public.

Followup Action

The law suit strategy was successful and would be used again, but the major activity of CBC was soon focused on the actual followup of complaints against nursing home operators. This direct client advocacy became the basis for CBC's activity. In the beginning, a telephone or written complaint about a home was followed up by a request to the city or State Health Department to investigate the situation. In some cases, CBC attempted to visit the home and to speak to the patient in question. This procedure led to two discoveries: (1) CBC frequently received no response from the health department on its request for an inspection, and (2) nursing home operators frequently denied access to persons affiliated with CBC.

In the fall of 1972, CBC once again turned to legal strategy and sued a home that had denied a CBC worker entrance. The court ruled in favor of CBC and permitted the unsolicited visit of nursing home advocates under certain conditions—for example, during normal visiting hours. In order to obtain follow-up to inspection requests, CBC suggested a rule change that would require state nursing home inspectors to file reports of their investigation of complaints within a reasonable time limit. CBC, aware that the act covering rule changes required public hearings, organized groups to support the suggested change at the rules hearing and to testify in support of its adoption. The rule requiring the prompt filing of reports was finally promulgated by the director of the state department and went into effect in 1973. CBC was now prepared to serve as a consumer advocacy organization on both the class and individual action level.

Development of Individual Client Advocacy

The handling of complaints was a rapidly growing activity. Chomet had devoted considerable amounts of his time to CBC and had led it through several court battles as president, but it was obvious that the client advocacy work would require full-time leadership. The initial major financing from the nation's first urban coalition, New Detroit, came two years after CBC was established. This funding was supplemented by similar donations from church groups and civic associations. It was soon possible to hire a full-time staff. The first employee was a young professional who was doing alternate service as part of his military obligation. The executive director's job was offered to Chomet a few months later, and he decided to leave his full-time professional position and accept it. The president's chair went to Frieda Gorrecht, a highly effective and militant administrator with a national reputation in planning and running services and activities for retired workers. She was closely affiliated with the United Automobile Workers union and had long been a leading spokesperson for concerns of the elderly in Detroit. She was well connected politically at the state and local levels. As the leader of consumer interests, she consistently urged the organization and its staff to take an aggressive and persistent stance. This stance was to prove a major asset of the consumer advocacy organization.

Structure

Together, Chomet and Gorrecht were able to structure and staff an advocacy operation. The telephones in the donated downtown office of CBC were handled by a combination of social work student field placements and public administrators, volunteer retired workers, and CBC staff persons. This volunteer and professional staff enabled the organization to establish a recordkeeping system for complaints. As a call was received, the nature of the complaint was recorded. In some cases, the complaint was trivial, or possibly a nuisance call was received. In most instances, however, serious problems were reported. A regular system of followup was devised which permitted accurate recordkeeping, but there was also a great deal of trial-by-error in the earliest days. Every complaint was followed up, however, and an accurate picture of conditions in nursing homes began to emerge.

Relationship of Client Advocacy to Class Action Advocacy

Several programs resulted from the client advocacy approach taken by CBC. This approach also became the basis for undertaking some class action cases that resulted in a substantial improvement in the living conditions of the elderly in nursing homes. A frequent complaint concerned operators of homes who were using the funds of their Medicaid patients, funds which were protected by law. Any person in a nursing home who is supported by state or federal assistance is entitled to retain a small amount of funds for his own use. It was discovered that nursing home operators were deducting such necessary items as laundry and tissues from these personal accounts. CBC undertook the investigation of this situation as a major activity. The administrative appeals route was once again used, this time through the State Department of Social Services which administered the Medicaid program. The department was reluctant to publish new rules about the protected income portion of Medicaid patients in nursing homes, and CBC considered suing the state director of the Department of Social Services to force him to comply with federal standards regarding protected income. After considerable pressure, the rules were finally promulgated which required operators to establish separate accounts for the protected funds of each individual patient and forbade the arbitrary deduction of operating expenses from these funds.

In another class action situation, the CBC investigators discovered that nursing home operators were notified by state inspectors when they would be conducting their annual licensing examination. The state argued that notification was necessary to assure that appropriate personnel and records would be available when the inspector arrived. CBC contended that prior announcement of inspections was one more example of the state's desire to protect the nursing home operator. (This claim must have been viewed with some irony by the state officials who had been accused by the operators for many years of being arbitrary and against the interests of private nursing homes.) CBC pursued the legislative route this time and asked the governor to write a law forbidding prior announcement of nursing home inspections. Since unannounced inspections had been the practice of the City of Detroit Department of Public Health for many years, the departure was not too radical. In the past, the state legislature had been very supportive of nursing home operators and, in turn, had been supported financially by the nursing home association. However, the growth of a consumer advocacy group made it politically less desirable to defend the nursing home interests, and some legislators began to express their own personal, frequently negative, experiences with nursing homes. In April 1974, the governor signed a law forbidding prior announcement of nursing home inspections.

Formalization of Advocacy Through an Ombudsman Approach

The most direct result of CBC's client advocacy work was the stimulation of similar programs in other areas through a federal project. In 1973, Congress had appropriated funds to establish a nursing home ombudsman demonstration program. (The term *ombudsman* derives from the title of the Norwegian official who intercedes on behalf of a citizen who has a grievance against a government-sponsored agency or provider.) In addition to ombudsmen in official positions in a number of selected states, Congress established experimental programs in 1973 based on the use of volunteers. CBC encouraged the National Council of Senior Citizens (NCSC), a membership organization with many retired union members, to apply for funding for such a program. NCSC received a grant from the U.S. Department of Health, Education, and Welfare in 1973 to establish a model ombudsman project in Michigan. Michigan was included as a model site, largely in recognition of the background work done by CBC and the close connection between NCSC and CBC board members. The grant required the establishment of ombudsman project offices in Washington, D.C., and in state capitals. In Michigan, an office was opened in Lansing, and activity centers were provided in the Upper Peninsula and in the southeast region of Michigan. CBC was subcontracted to handle the southeast center, and a separate office was established within CBC headquarters to maintain the distinct nature of the ombudsman project.

The activity began in July 1972 with the selection and training of senior citizen volunteers who would act as patient advocates in nursing homes. They were given information on the operation of nursing homes and were briefed on state and federal regulations. The patient advocates would visit a nursing home to talk with individuals who had complaints. If the operator failed to correct legitimate problems, the advocates would file a report which would be sent to the State Department of Public Health for appropriate action. In most cases, the advocates were able to resolve the situation by discussions with the nursing home operator. A number of operators welcomed the ombudsman project as a means of demonstrating their cooperative spirit and their willingness to meet the needs of their patients. The early concerns that the patient advocates would cause trouble over minor issues proved to be unfounded, for the senior citizens were well able to discriminate between minor or nuisance complaints and legitimate and remediable ones.

The ombudsman program developed an effective liaison with the State Department of Public Health. Chuck Waller, the executive director of the state operation in Lansing, was a trained social worker with an outgoing personality. He worked closely with state health officials and was able to resolve some very difficult problems as they arose during the early activities of the program. In addition, some state representatives asked Waller to write legislation covering a variety of issues. He introduced several dozen pieces of legislation, and two or three major measures were adopted into law. The ombudsman office in the state capital became a focal point for legislators who sought an alternative perspective on nursing home regulation. Waller provided an effective balance to the perspectives of the nursing home associations and the State Department of Public Health.

In Detroit, the United Automobile Workers viewed the CBC ombudsman operation as a success. They asked CBC to set up a patient advocacy program using union retirees. As a direct result of the law suit won by CBC regarding public disclosure of nursing home inspection reports, the Michigan Association of Regional Medical Programs funded CBC to operate Project Inform to provide information on how to use these reports. In addition, CBC's nursing home committees published a booklet entitled "How to Choose a Nursing Home," with the cooperation of the Institute of Gerontology at the University of Michigan and Wayne State University. By 1975 CBC had grown into an organization employing a staff of nine full-time workers operating three major programs. The annual budget had grown from about $10,000 in its first year to nearly $180,000 in its fifth year.

The Role of Advocacy in Policy-Making

The relationship between the consumer advocacy organization and the nursing home industry also changed during this period. In its first years, CBC was under constant attack from the nursing home industry. Although some operators felt that a consumer advocacy organization had a legitimate role in improving services, the official representatives of the industry sought to discredit CBC, or at least to limit its access to state officials and decision-makers. The executive director of the nursing home association was a former public relations agent and had good relationships with the press. He sought to characterize the industry as concerned with the well-being of sick, elderly persons. In contrast, he presented the state to the press as unfeeling and unconcerned about the elderly in nursing homes, seeking only to save money by shutting down homes. There were frequent running battles in the press between the state health department and the nursing home association.

CBC entered this interchange by issuing news releases on its findings through its patient advocacy work. It called press conferences to announce the law suits filed to open records to public inspection and to allow entry to nursing homes by consumer advocates. In time, the nursing home articles tended to become balanced between the views of the state, the industry, and the consumer advocate organization. This was probably the first indication that CBC was having a moderating effect on the nursing home situation. The level of debate rose from vindictive charges and countercharges to more balanced exchanges. CBC requested and was given representation on several statewide committees that had had largely industry representation. Persons affiliated with CBC served on the Advisory Committee on Nursing Homes in the State Department of Public Health and the Adult Services Advisory Committee of the Department of Social Services. In addition, CBC members served on several taskforces concerned with issues such as nursing home payments, level of care in nursing homes, and alternatives to long-term care. Representatives made substantial contributions, helping to provide a basis for cooperation with the industry and the regulators while maintaining the basic role of consumer advocate.

Other CBC Studies

CBC was originally chartered to deal with consumer problems in after-care facilities. In its early years, it concentrated on nursing home activities, but by 1973, it was prepared to pay serious attention to the problems of elderly persons outside nursing homes and to the nonelderly in nursing homes. A study conducted during 1970-1971 to examine the status of home health care indicated that only a small fraction of state and federal funds were being spent in Michigan on this alternative to institutional care. The study recommended that greater reliance be placed on it. This CBC effort has not achieved notable success, largely because home health care agencies have been unable to form an effective lobby. However, the study has been used as the basis for developing a home health care plan for the southeast Michigan Comprehensive Health Planning area.

Between 1973 and 1974, another CBC study examined the condition of after-care facilities in Michigan, with special reference to those that receive patients released from mental hospitals. In the early phase of the study, CBC discovered that the State Department of Mental Health, which was committed to releasing patients back into the community, refused to reveal the number of patients released and the nature of the after-care facilities that received them. The CBC study indicated that most of these facilities were poorly supervised and ill-prepared to meet the special needs of the newly released mental patient. CBC subsequently called for improved standards of care and increased training for operators of after-care facilities. This concern has become an ongoing activity for CBC, funded, in part, by a contract with the Southeastern Michigan Comprehensive Health Planning Council.

In a related study, also funded by the Planning Council, CBC investigated the zoning regulations that restrict the location of after-care facilities in many municipalities. It recommended a standard form of zoning ordinance and adequate planning to assure that after-care facilities benefit from good locations in normal community settings.

Internal Organization and Funding of an Advocacy Group

CBC's administrative structure enables it to undertake a variety of activities and still remain a highly credible performance record. The administrative core consists of the executive director, office manager, and secretary; they provide the continuity essential to any ongoing activity. The major research projects are staffed by full-time professionals who have degrees in social work or nursing. Most of the research since the beginning, however, has been performed by student field placements. Senior volunteers have played an important research role. They take complaints over the telephone and visit patients in nursing homes. The amount of training required is minimal, and quality control can be exercised over their activities.

The general membership plays an interesting role in CBC activities. At the annual meeting, the staff reports on recent activities, and officers and board members are elected. The monthly meetings present resolutions drawn up by the executive and by the standing and working committees. At these monthly meetings, the members give their reactions to positions taken or suggested by the staff and executive committee. The meetings are well attended and attract both retired persons and professionals who have an interest in nursing homes. In addition to standing committees, such as membership and bylaws committees, there are working committees in each of the major interest areas. The executive committee meets monthly and actively participates in decisions on the general direction of CBC.

Membership dues provide a base support of about $5,000 per year, but this amount barely covers the cost of a part-time bookkeeper. Hence, CBC has sought two types of funding: contributions and contracts. Contributions come mainly from church groups and occasionally from a private donor. CBC first approached funding sources established by the major givers in the Detroit area. They were given little encouragement, perhaps because of CBC's aggressive advocacy position and its frequent recourse to the courts. In order to allow for tax-exempt donations, CBC set up the Citizens for Better Care Institute which was authorized to work on educational and other activities with tax-exempt status. In spite of this effort, donations were still slow in coming and seldom amounted to more than 25 percent of CBC's operating budget. The majority of the funds came from grants and contracts for CBC research and advocacy projects.

The contract with the National Council of Senior Citizens to conduct the ombudsman program in southeast Michigan was the first major grant. A working relationship with Wayne County commissioners resulted in the award of a contract by the Southeastern Michigan Comprehensive Health Planning Council to report on the condition of placement facilities for patients released from mental hospitals. In addition, CBC has received contracts from the Planning Council to complete specialized studies.

The CBC leadership has actively followed up on the opportunities it has helped to create. The best example is the proposal to develop an information service that would more effectively utilize the nursing home inspection reports made public by CBC legal action. As a result of these grants, CBC now operates at a budget of nearly $250,000 per year; this level of funding can be expected to continue for several more years.

Assessment of Advocacy Effectiveness

In assessing the impact of Citizens for Better Care, it is necessary to separate its class action from its individual action type of advocacy. Both types benefit the elderly patient in nursing homes, but they are different in scope, method, and impact. The class action type undertaken by CBC has been particularly effective, winning praise in newspaper editorials and resulting in consulting requests by planning and regulatory bodies. The organization is taken seriously: it has access to the media and apparently has the ear of important policy-makers and legislators. CBC's reports are carefully researched, accurate, and readable, and have had considerable impact on decisions relating to home health care, facilities for the released mental patient, zoning regulations for after-care facilities, and the like.

CBC has also been effective in gaining support for tighter controls on nursing home profits and in publicizing possible conflict of interest by some state health department employees. It has high visibility in southeast Michigan and is steadily gaining support in the rest of the state. While its legislative record has been limited, it is increasing. Since CBC has seldom worked actively for a particular piece of legislation, it is difficult to measure its effectiveness in lobbying. However, its track record is good, and it is recognized as an organization that produces reliable material.

It is more difficult to measure CBC's impact on the quality of care in nursing homes. Since this is the organization's primary responsibility, it would be useful to have an assessment, but there are few measures that can be used. CBC's complaints division handles hundreds of calls a year and has an efficient system of recordkeeping and followup. The ombudsman program it supervises has provided senior citizen advocates who actively pursue and attempt to resolve the problems of individual patients. The quality of care in nursing homes has risen since CBC was formed, but upgraded care is part of a nationwide trend. In Michigan, the individual advocacy of CBC has certainly provided some incentive for this improvement.

Contributions of CBC

CBC has made at least four major contributions as an advocacy organization: (1) it has produced useful studies, (2) it has mobilized resources on behalf of nursing home patients, (3) it has initiated and followed up on action programs to improve services in nursing homes, and (4) it has served as a check on the formal regulatory functions of government. These achievements have been the result of a carefully constructed strategy that deliberately seeks limited areas for advocacy and pursues these areas carefully. CBC has proven to be a persistent organization and, given the time required to make progress in consumer advocacy, this persistence has been an essential element in its success. In addition, CBC has consistently striven for accuracy in its public statements. It has thereby gained a reputation for credibility that has enhanced its effectiveness. The four contributions of study, mobilization, action, and feedback have made CBC a useful model for other consumer advocacy groups.

CBC has also made contributions to planning and service delivery functions. In terms of planning, advocacy groups can provide a counterbalance to the perspectives of both the planners and the providers of health services. An advocacy organization consistently looks at a situation from the consumer's viewpoint, thus producing useful information and insights into long-range planning. If the research and analysis of the advocacy group are well prepared, they may be considered as the basis for planning improved programs. In terms of service delivery systems, advocacy groups serve to improve the quality of care and to contain costs by looking carefully for poor care and cost overruns. Through followup for individual complaints, they also serve as a check on the providers of services. This contribution is most effective where there is a recordkeeping system that allows the accumulated data to be translated into recommendations for remedial action.

CBC's most important contribution, however, has been its ability to effect permanent changes in the administrative and legislative functions that regulate health care providers. The use of the judicial process is admittedly harsh and unfriendly, *but taking providers and, in some cases, regulators to court is an effective way of getting their attention*. Individual consumer advocacy has only a limited and short-lived effect on the delivery system. It resolves some inequities but must be continuously repeated to assure the elimination of abuses against individuals. Individual followup in the form of a complaint bureau or an ombudsman program is useful since both provide the cumulative data needed to advocate for more permanent change.

It is class action or institutional advocacy, however, that forces changes in the behavior of provider and regulatory organizations. Through their efforts to open up the process, institutional advocates force participants in the service delivery system into higher levels of accountability and performance. The role of the institutional advocate is not to educate the consumer as to the best way to use the delivery system; that function should be performed by providers and regulators. The critic's role of the advocate is annoying, but it is ultimately most effective. In the case of CBC, it has combined individual advocacy with followup and action at the institutional level. Consumer advocacy differs from consumer participation by taking an adversary, rather than a collaborative, role. As such, it makes a special contribution to the improvement of services for elderly consumers.

Reports Prepared and Published by Citizens for Better Care

Home Health Services for the Aged in Southeast Michigan
Aftercare Facilities in Michigan
A Survey of Selected Aftercare Facilities in Wayne County
Day Care Centers for the Elderly
The Certification Program for Mentally Retarded and Mentally Ill Nursing Care in Michigan Nursing Homes
Nursing Home Regulation: Description and Recommendations
The Role of Government Agencies in the Nursing Home Field
Governmental Nursing Home Planning in Wayne County
Information, Referral and Ombudsman Services Needed for Wayne County Nursing Home Patients
How to Choose a Nursing Home

These reports may be obtained by writing to Citizens for Better Care, 960 East Jefferson, Detroit, Michigan 48207.

12

THE SOUTH CAROLINA NURSING HOME OMBUDSMAN PROJECT

William V. Bradley

The term *ombudsman* is relatively new to the United States. The nursing home ombudsman is an even newer concept. The nursing home ombudsman projects, the first national demonstration of health-related ombudsman activities in the United States, were initially proposed in a speech made by President Richard Nixon before the American Association of Retired Persons and National Retired Teachers Association on June 25, 1971. On that occasion, the president said, "If there is any single institution in this country that symbolizes the tragic isolation and the shameful neglect of older Americans, it is the substandard nursing home."

Several weeks later, on August 6, 1971, the president noted that many nursing homes in this country were far short of complying with the standards set by the Department of Health, Education, and Welfare. In this speech, the president announced his eight-point plan to improve the quality of nursing home care. He directed HEW to establish investigative units that would respond constructively to complaints made by or on behalf of individual nursing home patients. In the spring of 1972, letters were sent to the governors of all fifty states, to the District of Columbia, and to national associations representing older persons, inviting them to submit proposals for establishing nursing home ombudsman officers. To qualify for an ombudsman project an organization had to satisfy three requirements: to become informed of the conditions under which nursing home patients lived; to take appropriate action to resolve the problems identified in the area of long-term care; to receive, respond to, and resolve complaints made by or on behalf of nursing home patients.

On June 30, 1972, the Health Services and Mental Health Administration awarded five contracts. Four were to the state governments of Idaho, Pennsylvania, South Carolina, and Wisconsin to establish a state ombudsman office linked to a local unit of government. The fifth was awarded to the National Council of Senior Citizens to test the effectiveness of a nursing home ombudsman project operating independently of government jurisdiction and to study the feasibility of linking a national volunteer organization to state and local volunteer units. The National Council of Senior Citizens selected Michigan as the site for its demonstration program. The nursing home ombudsman projects remained under the Health Services and Mental Health Administration until early 1973 when the nursing home ombudsman project was transferred to the Administration on Aging (AoA). The AoA staff responsible for nursing homes assumed responsibility for administering the project during its third year.

Each of the five projects was located in different levels of state government. The project for Wisconsin was located in the lieutenant governor's office. That for Idaho was in the office of aging. (In Idaho, this office is not a separate agency; it acts, more or less, as a planning office under the auspices of the governor.) In Pennsylvania, the project was located within the State Department of Public Health, the Department of Social Services, and the Aging Department, which form one large agency; therefore, Pennsylvania's project is several layers down in the bureaucracy. In South Carolina, the project was placed with the Commission on Aging, which is a separate agency within the state. The Michigan project, a totally voluntary project under the auspices of the National Council of Senior Citizens which has no governmental control, was the only nongovernmental project among the five. Placing each project in a different setting provided the government information for making a choice on how permanent projects would be set up. The remainder of this chapter will deal with the activities of the ombudsman project as it was established in South Carolina.

In July 1972, the South Carolina Commission on Aging received a request for proposal to conduct a nursing home ombudsman project in South Carolina. In August 1972, the commission hired a director who was given the title of state ombudsman. In October, the remainder of the staff was selected. The project started with three professionals—the state ombudsman, an assistant ombudsman, and a local ombudsman—and one secretary. The local ombudsman was in charge of a four-county area near the central midlands in the state. By placing an ombudsman in a small, concentrated area, the South Carolina project attempted to perform a demonstration within a demonstration. At the beginning of the project, there were approximately 7,500 skilled- and intermediate-care nursing beds in the state. Of this total, approximately 1,200 to 1,400 were located in the central midlands. This area contains a cross-section of the urban and rural populations of the state as well as a cross-section of skilled- and intermediate-care beds. By limiting the local program to a four-county area, the local ombudsman was better able to serve the clients by responding more readily to problems.

The federal government provided no guidelines for starting ombudsman projects. South Carolina chose to begin with a random sampling of all nursing home patients in the state before actually beginning field operations. Each of the three ombudsmen was assigned a territory, and every nursing home in the state was visited. Patients were interviewed and were asked specific questions concerning the care and treatment they were receiving in the homes. This pretest revealed that most patients in nursing homes could not relate their needs since most of them were infirm or senile and could not communicate. As the project progressed, it was soon discovered that approximately 95 percent of all problems and complaints originated from the patient's friends or relatives or from the staff, with most coming from the relatives. The pretest visits lasted until January 1973. At this time, an intensive advertising and publicity program began. Newspaper releases, TV spots, and radio interviews were used to publicize the fact that the commission was now ready to receive complaints through its ombudsman program. The more intense the publicity, the more complaints were received. This fact was not surprising, for just as most businesses that depend on advertising get increased business from a high concentration of advertising, so the response to the ombudsman program accelerated. Publicity and advertising are important components of a nursing home ombudsman program.

Organization of the Program

During the first year, the problems and complaints centered on either the skilled- or intermediate-care nursing homes. No one could foresee the avalanche of complaints that would be received.

A rather large Advisory Committee was formed for the South Carolina ombudsman project. Each person or agency selected for the committee represented an area of interest and experience that could advise the ombudsman project. Agencies represented on the committee were the Department of Health and Environmental Control, the Department of Social Services, the Social Security Administration, representatives from the Nurses Association, the Licensed Practical Nurses Association, the Retired Teachers Association, the Pharmaceutical Association, and consumers at large.

As part of the planning, the ombudsman program staff met with federal representatives from the region. Even though the project was funded directly from Washington, it was felt that contacts within the region would also be necessary. Therefore, a meeting was held with representatives from the Social Security Administration, Social and Rehabilitative Services, the Bureau of Health Insurance, and several other agencies within the long-term care division of the region. The contact within the region proved most helpful in the ongoing conduct of the program. Because it had sometimes been difficult to get answers to questions from state agencies, having a contact person within the region helped resolve many problems.

As the project grew and expanded, problems emerged and, with the start of Supplemental Security Income (SSI), contacts within regional offices proved even more helpful, particularly since South Carolina used the same guidelines for Medicaid eligibility as SSI used.

The regional contacts also proved helpful in the state ombudsman's meetings within the region sponsored by HEW. At these meetings, the ombudsman met people within the region who could help resolve some of the day-to-day problems. Regional contacts also made the project more personal since the ombudsman could sit down and talk informally with people from regional offices who also were interested in the program.

Exposure at regional and national meetings proved to be helpful to the state ombudsman. As a result, he was selected to serve on several national committees to help determine rules and regulations for nursing home operations, and on a committee for curriculum development for the nursing home surveyors' training program conducted by Tulane University.

The state ombudsman is a member of several state health-related committees so that he can keep abreast of conditions in nursing homes and of developments in long-term care. He also serves as a resource person for the Legislative Committee on Aging, a committee composed of members from the State House and Senate and consumers. Through this committee, legislation was passed giving the ombudsman statutory authority to go into nursing homes or agencies to investigate complaints. This legislation was passed during the first year of the program's operation. South Carolina has been the only state to pass this legislation.

The ombudsman was instrumental in the enactment of the State Adult Abuse and Protective Services Law; a law requiring skilled- and intermediate-care facilities to itemize their patients' statements; and a bill requiring boarding homes to itemize statements of charges to their residents.

Regulatory Agencies in South Carolina

Two agencies in South Carolina are responsible for most of the programs that affect nursing homes: (1) the Department of Health and Environmental Control, which is charged with licensing and certifying all health facilities in the state; and (2) the Department of Social Services, which is a single state agency for the Medicaid Title XIX program. The state ombudsman works very closely with these two agencies in carrying out day-to-day activities. The Department of Health and Environmental Control, acting as a regulatory agency, has nurses, pharmacists, dietitians, and other staff with expertise in the health field. This staff is readily available to the ombudsman and is called on quite frequently to aid in investigating complaints. The dietitian is most helpful when a complaint concerns a therapeutic diet or some other special diet that has been ordered by the attending physician. The medical review team from the Department of Social Services discusses their findings with the ombudsman from time to time. The ombudsman also acts as a liaison between these two agencies, since in many programs there are certain gray areas that require a third party.

The relationship between the regulatory and other supportive agencies within the state has been vital to the success of the ombudsman program as it has operated in South Carolina. Any state starting an ombudsman project should develop these relationships very early in their programs.

Scope of the Project

The project is now in its third year of operation, and each year its scope has expanded. In its first year, the project was concerned primarily with nursing homes, both skilled and intermediate. In the following year, boarding homes were added. At present, the project's concern encompasses nursing homes, mental hospitals, mental retardation institutions, boarding homes, and other long-term care facilities, with an emphasis on nursing and boarding homes. The project has responded to requests for denial of Medicare, Medicaid, and SSI benefits. The SSI benefits are of particular importance as they determine whether an individual qualifies for Medicaid. In South Carolina, the Medicaid program pays for nursing home care 365 days a year; it is imperative that low-income people receive these benefits.

Since the program is located in the Commission on Aging, many health-related problems are now being referred to the state ombudsman. The commission is charged by law to carry on an advocacy program for the aging. The nursing home ombudsman program is located in the Commission on Aging because approximately 95 percent of all residents in nursing homes are sixty-five years of age and over. The average age of nursing home patients in South Carolina is eighty-three.

The ombudsman's office is located in Columbia, the state capital. Since South Carolina is a relatively small state, it does not have the geographical problems of the larger states. The capital is situated in the geographic center, thereby facilitating the ombudsman's access to nursing homes by automobile.

The nursing home ombudsman has achieved a high level of visibility throughout the state. This was particularly true in the early stages of the program. The state ombudsman attracted a lot of attention since the ombudsman idea was very new to most residents of the state. The news media in particular liked the idea; thus, getting air time for the program was easily achieved. Several interviews were on prime time evening news shows, and all the major newspapers in the state carried feature articles on the program. Publicity was the lifeblood of the program in its early days; today the program has reached the grass roots level. Many of the patients know the ombudsman personally, or their families have heard about the program and do not hesitate to call when they have a problem.

Accomplishments of the Program

The major accomplishments of the program in South Carolina include the enactment of the State Adult Abuse and Protective Services Law, supportive legislation requiring cooperation from nursing and boarding homes, and legislation providing the ombudsman office with authority to investigate the records of nursing facilities and to review agency records; and a cooperative position paper from the South Carolina Commission on Aging regarding the state's policy for discharging and payment for non-Medicaid patients released from state mental hospitals. The ombudsman program has also pursuaded state agencies to fill social service gaps in appropriate programs and has been instrumental in getting the Department of Social Services to update and strengthen the regulations for boarding homes. The ombudsman has mediated several conflicts between state agencies and has been appointed to several policy-making committees in the state.

Case Histories

Among the program's most meaningful accomplishments are the resolutions of the individual patients' problems. In one well-remembered case, a lady's children were trying to have her declared mentally incompetent in order to acquire her assets. The case began with the ombudsman's receipt of a short letter written in a very even hand; the lady in question was simply asking for a visit because she wanted to leave her nursing home and return to her home. The ombudsman went to the nursing home and talked with the patient personally; she told him that she was being held at the nursing home, despite the fact that her doctor had discharged her as a patient. The ombudsman contacted the attending physician who stated that the lady could indeed go home and was capable of an independent living.

Meanwhile, the family initiated papers in another town to have their mother declared mentally incompetent. The ombudsman then advised the patient to seek legal counsel. The ombudsman himself contacted an attorney for her. The attorney had her examined by two doctors who agreed with the attending physician that she was both physically and mentally competent and should be discharged. The case went to court, and the judge ruled in favor of the patient. Today this patient still performs her household chores, does her own shopping and cooking, and manages quite well. Had it not been for the ombudsman, this lady may well have remained in an institution the rest of her live.

The ombudsman program does not limit its activities to individuals. Another rewarding case involved a boarding home that had operated for many years as the old county home. The residents were satisfied and were well taken care of. The home was clean and warm, and they received a balanced diet and good medical care. There was one problem, however: federal law states that residents of a home controlled by a city, county, or state government are not entitled to receive SSI checks. In this particular case, there was no way the county could obtain the funds to subsidize thirty-one residents.

The chairman of the board of trustees of the home, the ombudsman, and other board and county council members met on several occasions to find a way the home could continue to operate. After several meetings, the county council agreed to pass an ordinance permitting the home's board of trustees to operate the home as a nonprofit organization with no government controls. The battle took more than a year to win, but the thirty-one people still have a home.

The ombudsman's job can be very exasperating. Besides dealing with the bureaucracy, he frequently has to make very personal decisions. For example, he must decide whether there are guilt feelings within the family because they cannot take care of their relative in their own homes. In these difficult and often emotional circumstances, it is not easy to reason with a family.

The decisions that have to be reached in each case must be in the patient's best interests. In one case, the ombudsman had to insist on what he thought was best for the patient: to place the patient in a state institution. This decision was not well received by the family. The ombudsman had accumulated much detailed information on the case, talked with the attending physician, and agreed with him that the patient required institutional care. The family had to be convinced that she needed treatment and that the state hospital was the best facility for her.

The state hospital in South Carolina has a long-term nursing care unit located on a campus away from the main hospital where patients may be transferred after a thirty-day observation period. The ombudsman persuaded the family that, after the observation period and the delivery of recommended treatment, the patient could be transferred to this nursing home. The family visited several times during the observation period and continued to be most upset that their sister was at the state hospital. After the observation period was over, the ombudsman talked with the psychiatrist, the social worker, and the administrator of the nursing home and made arrangements for the patient to be transferred to the nursing home. The family now visits her there. The patient is doing very well, has responded to treatment, and the family is satisfied. Again, it was a case of making a decision about what was best for the patient and convincing the family.

These are some of the easy cases. The more difficult ones involve problems such as whether a call light was answered last week, or whether the food was cold on a certain day. In a nursing home, no two complaints are the same. Since individuals and different nursing homes located in different parts of the state are involved, each case presents a unique problem. Thus, when investigating a complaint, the ombudsman must look at each complaint separately. Even though he may have received a complaint about a home in the past, each time an investigation is made the complaint should be investigated as an entirely new case. Most administrators try to do a good job; hence, it is important for the ombudsman not to project a negative attitude. An open mind is crucial in investigating any type of complaint.

The South Carolina program and the other four demonstration projects have proven successful. Nationally, the five original projects (and two others which were added after the beginning of the second year) were all demonstration projects. Legislation has been introduced which proposes to set up HEW ombudsman in all states; this legislation is presently in committee. Based on the program's success, the AoA is currently providing additional funds to set up ombudsman programs in all states.

13

THE MICHIGAN OMBUDSMAN PROGRAM

Charles H. Waller, Jr.

The typical institutionalized aged person is a widow and seventy-five years of age or older, has no family or a scattered family, has more than one concurrent diagnosis, and is at least partially dependent on public assistance.

In nine of eleven instances, the nursing home is a privately owned facility operated for profit and therefore does not have an accountability to the community such as a board of trustees has. The owner's previous background or experience is not usually related to the institutional care of the aged. The home typically has no resident medical staff and only a limited number of professional health care personnel. The personnel are predominantly unskilled, undertrained, and uncommitted. If any use is made of volunteers (and only the exceptional home does), these are generally untrained teenagers.

The total public community has board responsibility in the area of nursing homes in that more than two out of every three dollars that go to nursing homes are public dollars. Public agencies in most communities have insufficient staff help to perform the many responsibilities involved in the standards, regulation, and reimbursement of nursing homes. Typically, there are numerous nursing home facilities spread out over a wide area; monitoring is limited and difficult.

Thus, the basic problem in nursing homes today is that the average patient is lonely, dependent, and withdrawn; excluded from community life; and confined to an institution remote from the mainstream of health care and life, with no recourse other than an overburdened public agency whose monitoring functions are made difficult by the many dispersed facilities. With so little regulation of the industry, it is not surprising that countless thousands of nursing home patients now live under conditions that sap them of the will to live and that result in malnutrition, dehydration, oversedation, and neglect—if not abject abuse.

A Solution to the Problem: NHOP

A solution requires massive action on many fronts. One such action is the Nursing Home Ombudsman Project of Michigan (NHOP), a program developed in 1972 to provide a means by which patients or persons acting on their behalf can make known their legitimate complaints, such as their isolation or the poor quality of care; and by which attempts can be made to redress these grievances on a person-to-person basis.

An ombudsman program cannot solve the basic problem that exists. An ombudsman cannot create high-quality facilities where none exist; he cannot take over the inspection and regulatory functions of governmental agencies; and he is not a coordinator of existing services. His job is to solve grievances and thereby improve the quality of services provided by others; to determine areas where the current system (including aspects controlled by the government, nursing homes, and medical profession) is not responsive to patients' needs; and to try to set in motion the means for change.

The NHOP of Michigan is under contract with the National Council of Senior Citizens and the Health Services and Mental Health Administration, Public Health Service. Since its inception, the program has demonstrated that an ombudsman (or consumer advocate) can achieve improvements in nursing home care in a way no one else can. He can listen to a patient's complaint and then attempt to resolve the problem simply by conferring with the nursing home owner or administrator, arguing persuasively for voluntary correction of a situation. Only if this personal contact fails does he resort to regulatory agencies or adverse publicity. The ombudsman can alert responsible authorities to problems that otherwise might go unnoticed. He can do this most persuasively when he is linked to and backed up by a large membership organization with voting power and with local, state, and national voices raised on behalf of consumers.

Among the purposes of the NHOP of Michigan are to determine the effectiveness of volunteers, especially retirees, in the role of consumer advocates and to test procedures for directing the work of the volunteers. In the past, the role of volunteers in nursing homes has been limited to "friendly visiting," and volunteers have been cautioned to avoid criticizing the nursing home or the care received. The Michigan program is one of the first to give the volunteer a different function: to solicit complaints from patients, assess the validity of the complaints, and attempt to resolve them. To enable volunteers to perform this function, they are instructed in the rules and regulations governing nursing homes and in the conditions to inspect so that they can accurately determine where problems exist. The first training program lasted one week, and while it was considered a success, it was too long. Hence, the second training program was scheduled for only two days. In its third year, the program tried other training methods, such as allowing newly recruited volunteers to accompany experienced volunteers on their rounds. New training methods and additional funds have allowed the program to be expanded into new areas and effective training to be provided at minimal expense.

Project Structure, Organization, Placement, and Relationships

The project is located in Lansing, the state capital. The state legislature, the Michigan Departments of Public Health, Mental Health, Social Services, and Licensing and Regulation, the Office of Services to the Aging, the Health Care Association of Michigan (Profit Nursing Homes), Michigan Non-Profit Homes Association, and other organizations involved in health care also have their main offices there. Lansing is located in the middle of the Lower Peninsula, thereby allowing relatively easy access to any point in the state. Michigan's population centers, such as Detroit, Flint, Grand Rapids, and Kalamazoo, are all within an hour's or two hours' drive.

In operating the program, the Detroit office handles the tricounty Detroit area where over 100 of the state's 400 nursing homes are located. The Menominee office covers the entire Upper Peninsula, and the Lansing office covers the remainder of the state.

Scope of the Project

While the original project proposal was limited to nursing homes, issues involving mental hosptials and institutions, room and board homes, adult foster care facilities, county long-term care facilities, and hospitals have also been handled. Any and all problems of any resident, relative, friend, or staff person are dealt with, regardless of their ages. Noninstitutionalized individuals are also helped, particularly with remaining in their own homes rather than being institutionalized. Project staff members work closely with other state and local agencies in promoting and establishing services to keep the elderly in their own homes for as long as possible.

The ombudsman services should be flexible. They should be mainly involved with health care and satisfaction of the institutionalized resident. However, they should also have sufficient knowledge of agencies and resources to be able to assist those out of institutions with their health care needs—to deal with concerns on an individual basis as well as legislatively and in cooperation with other agencies.

Areas of Concern

According to the original contract, the prime areas of concern were the tricounty Detroit area, the tricounty Menominee area, and the tricounty Lansing area. However, the Menominee office, as previously stated, oversees concerns anywhere in the Upper Peninsula. The Lansing office handles all other problems outside the target areas. Ombudsman units have recently been established under the supervision of the Lansing office for two additional areas. Washtenaw and Kent counties. Future plans are to establish ombudsman units in other counties where there are high concentrations of nursing care facilities, such as Flint, Saginaw, Kalamazoo, Muskegon, Niles, Houghton, and Sault Ste. Marie.

The Kent County office has been established in conjunction with two colleges in the area. Student ombudsmen are under the direct supervision of a faculty member.

In Washtenaw County, the ombudsman unit utilizes both student and senior citizen volunteers. The County Office on Aging and the Washtenaw Community Mental Health Board supervise the operation. Students from area universities are under the supervision of their local schools. Volunteers file reports regularly, and personal contacts with the Lansing staff are frequent, as the state director of NHOP resides in the county.

Thus far, the state ombudsman and the local university directors themselves have been able to resolve the majority of problems. In cases where resolutions are impossible, the state director steps in to assist.

Based on its statewide operations since 1972 and its collection of complaints since that time, the Michigan ombudsman project has found significant differences between the urban and rural areas in Michigan.

The following overview lists data NHOP collected from 1972 to 1975 on some of the problem areas.

INFORMATION AND REFERRAL—COMPLAINT-BASED

Categories:

1. Quality of institutional life
2. Formalized programs
3. Lack of professional/technical services
4. Quality of professional/technical services
5. Finances
6. Legal problems
7. Nursing home administration; rules, regulations, policy
8. Diet
9. Physical facilities
10. Regulatory and/or service agency
11. Other

Problems and approaches differ from area to area. For example, the rural (Menominee Unit) volunteers can use a more informal approach to complaint resolution. Whereas the urban (Detroit, Lansing, Kent, Washtenaw) volunteers are usually "strangers" to the facility to which they are assigned as ombudsmen, the rural volunteers frequently have known many of the residents and personnel in the facilities they visit for most of their lives. They also know many of the local service agency personnel with whom they need to deal in resolving complaints. Thus, the rural volunteers can build their approach based on more casual relationships that have already been established. Geographic-

TOTAL URBAN CONCERNS HANDLED 1974-1975—334
TOTAL RURAL CONCERNS HANDLED 1973-1975—824

	Urban (Pct.)	Rural (Pct.)
1	11	8
2	2	5
3	16	15
4	13	9
5	5	6
6	4	3
7	11	6
8	18	5
9	10	20
10	3	5
11	7	17

ally, the rural area is much more difficult to cover than the urban. There are only a few facilities, but they are separated by hundreds of miles of sparsely populated areas, with the main roads often impassable in the winter and early spring months because of the severe climate conditions (snow in winter and mud in spring).

External Linkages

The Lansing office functions on two levels: as a local ombudsman unit with volunteers, and as a statewide agency representing the nursing home resident on long-term care issues. The goals are to alert the government regulators to concerns for better care and to press for legislative and regulatory changes, when needed.

The Lansing office serves as a link between the other units and the state government and other groups concerned with long-term care. Therefore, specific working agreements with state agencies and groups have been essential to its functions and operations.

Relationships established with numerous state representatives and senators have been most beneficial in getting legislation passed. The Lansing office's ability to resolve problems both for individuals and groups, has been aided by its working relationships with state agencies such as the Department of Public Health and its Bureau of Health Facilities and Health Care Administration; the Department of Social Services and its Bureaus of Medical Assistance, Medicaid-Fiscal Management Division, Policy and Planning, and Provider and Recipient Services; the Department of Mental Health; Office of Services to the Aging; Office of the Attorney General; Michigan Department of Licensing and Regulation and its Boards of Nursing, Pharmacy, Nursing Home Administrators, and Social Workers; the Health Care Association of Michigan and the Michigan Non-Profit Homes Association.

No agencies have been totally uncooperative. Some tend to be bogged down by bureaucratic details that hamper the prompt resolution of concerns. For the most part, however, the relations with these agencies have been extremely beneficial.

Other agencies, both statewide and local, with which the Lansing unit has had the most frequent contacts are: the Tri-County Office on Aging (Lansing); Michigan Nurses Association; Michigan League for Nursing; Capital Area Comprehensive Health Planning Association; Michigan Association of Regional Medical Programs; Michigan League for Human Services; Michigan State University Volunteer Bureau; Michigan State University Chronic Disease Module; American Association of Retired Persons (Lansing chapters); United Auto Workers retiree chapters; county councils on aging/county offices on aging; Institute of Gerontology, University of Michigan; Eastern Michigan University; Wayne State University; Michigan State University; Grand Valley State College; Grand Rapids Junior College; Northern Michigan University; Lansing Community College; and county offices of the Departments of Social Services, Public Health and Mental Health; church groups; and organized senior citizens' groups.

A state ombudsman agency's most critical working relationships are with the state legislature and with regulatory and licensing agencies involved in long-term care. These are of prime importance in obtaining legislative and regulatory changes and in resolving individual concerns. Knowledge of the structures of the State Departments of Public Health, Mental Health, and Social Services, and of where the power lies in each is imperative.

In terms of volunteer services, good relationships with colleges and universities and with organized senior citizens' groups are essential.

At the time NHOP began, the staff decided that the Lansing office's major goal would be the prompt resolution of the individual concerns of nursing home residents, particularly when these problems involve state regulatory agencies.

In dealing with state agencies that generally tend to be bureaucratic mazes, working relationships are established with those individuals who are less likely to be bound by departmental rules. That is, the bureau and division chiefs rather than a gamut of assistants are contacted. The relationships established with these individuals have been informal. The Lansing office delivers any complaints personally to the bureau chiefs and foregoes the formality of filing written complaints. The chiefs themselves resolve the concerns or they refer the complaints to the staff member(s) best able to handle them. As a result of this procedure, concerns have most often met with prompt resolution.

All too often, an individual consumer's confrontation with a state agency leads to countless referrals, wrong information, and frustration. Many times, too, individuals will not even attempt to seek an answer to their problems, mainly because they simply do not know to which organization they should turn. The Lansing office of NHOP has attempted to be that agency. It has tried to cut through the red tape and has found success with informal relationships.

The Staffing Pattern

The NHOP in Michigan has seven staff members and several volunteers. Staffing an ombudsman program in a state similar to Michigan would require an analysis of how the nursing care facilities and population centers are distributed throughout the state. An office in the state capital is essential for legislative and regulatory changes and contacts. At least three offices are necessary, each of which should have a local director, assistant, clerical staff, and an individual to supervise legislative and regulatory reform and additional ombudsman volunteer units.

The professionals should have some legal background, an understanding of the problems of the elderly, and a knowledge of the laws and regulations governing nursing care facilities.

Volunteers function most effectively as the links between the ombudsman offices and the nursing home residents. Their primary functions are to solicit complaints, verifying and resolving them within the confines of the nursing home.

Participation in Policy-Making Boards and Committees

Committee and board memberships include the Department of Licensing and Regulation—Board of Nursing home Administrators and consultant to the Board of Social Workers; Michigan Committee on Long-Term Care; special consultant to the House and Senate on Long-Term Care Issues; House Study Committee on Community Placement; National Association of Social Workers—Project Provide—Planning Committees, national and local; University of Michigan Faculty Academic Advisory Committee; Eastern Michigan University Advisory Council on Title I, II, and III Programming; Lansing Community College Advisory Council for Senior Adults; Governor's Consumer Conference—Planning Committee; Michigan Association of Regional Medical Programs—Project Review Committees; Office of Services to the Aging—Task Force on Health Care; Office of Services to the Aging—Task Force on Consumer Protection; Washtenaw County—RSVP Advisory Board, Mental Health Board, and Consortium; and Ypsilanti Council on Aging—commissioner. The most important committee or position would probably be that of consultant to the legislature on long-term care issues. The consultant has been most helpful in resolving issues of legislative reform. The member of the board regulating nursing home administrators is also of great importance because of his direct impact on the licensing standards and testing of administrators.

The low-level quality of care that aides and orderlies in nursing homes provide and the minimal (or sometimes nonexistent) amount of training they have received have been of almost universal concern among health care professionals. Michigan is now making an intense study of all aspects of the program—e.g., poor working conditions, inadequate or total absence of formal training programs, lack of job incentives, and low pay scales. NHOP is actively involved in the study. The Lansing unit staff has compiled information on all training programs for aides available in Michigan's community colleges, junior colleges, business schools, high schools, and other educational institutions. A report summarizing the findings has been written and will be used as the basis for designing a standard curriculum for statewide implementation.

The value of direct participation by the ombudsman program in the policy-making functions of boards and committees directly involved in the area of long-term care is difficult to assess. The creation of public policy is not as important—or as difficult—as is the attempt to enforce currently existing policy. Overall, Michigan has excellent standards on long-term care facilities and administrators. Where the problem comes in is enforcing these "model" standards. In Michigan's case, the current enforcement system is so tightly entwined with the nursing home industry itself that enforcement is more often than not ineffective. Michigan's standards may be superior to those of a majority of states, but the state is a long way from throwing off the domination of the nursing home industry.

Management of Complaints

In 1972, when the ombudsman project began, HEW and Macro Systems designed a six-page complaint form which was to be used by all projects to insure uniform data collection. The various ombudsman staffs, however, objected to its length and questioned its value in the resolution process; as a result, the form was scrapped. Each state project was thus left to its own devices in creating a workable documentation system.

The Detroit volunteers found that filing "formal" complaint reports is most effective in recording the volume of work handled by the Detroit office.

The rural volunteers, accustomed to a totally different lifestyle than their urban counterparts, file fewer formal complaint reports. The reasons are that there are fewer rural than urban volunteers; there are not as many facilities in rural areas; rural climatic conditions are more severe; and the more informal and personal relationships between the volunteers and nursing home residents and personnel in the rural areas makes formal complaints less necessary.

While formal complaints are not as plentiful in rural areas, their ombudsmen file daily reports. They record, in narrative form, the details of each visit made to a nursing home in their territory. These reports contain the history and resolution of the formal complaints filed as well as the innumerable smaller issues which the volunteers handle daily but do not feel need be added to the "formal" complaint category.

Major Factors Affecting the Volume and Nature of Complaints

Geographical location affects the nature of the complaints received. The Upper Peninsula health care facilities are frequently large old houses or hotels that have been converted to accommodate nursing care patients. Thus, complaints about physical plant deficiencies are common. The atmosphere in these facilities, however, is generally warm and homelike, and the care is more personal than that in larger facilities, for many of the Upper Peninsula facilities are operated as family businesses. The owner and administrator frequently are one and the same person, and in some instances, the owner and his family live in part of the facility. This situation is quite unlike that in urban areas, where facilities are newer and larger and have corporate ownership and hired administrators/financial managers.

Before NHOP came to Lansing, the mid-Michigan area had no effective mechanism for resolving the complaints of residents of health care facilities. The original NHOP technical proposal did not view the Lansing office as a unit for investigating complaints. However, because the area lacked an effective mechanism and because so very many complaints were being received, it soon became clear that a volunteer unit had to be established within the Lansing office.

The manner in which complaints have been handled have created a climate where nursing home administrators frequently request the assistance of the ombudsman in handling "difficult" residents or families. State departmental employees often turn to NHOP for help on issues that are outside their juris-diction.

Publicity for the project has been minimal because of the limited size of the Lansing unit staff. Every newspaper article, television or radio spot, and speaking engagement has resulted in an increase volume of complaints to the office, adding to the already excessive workload of the staff. On the positive side, publicity has brought volunteers to the program, and they are now being utilized to resolve some of the complaints referred to the office or solicited in their regular visits to nursing homes. The Lansing unit continues to prefer a low-keyed operation, however, and thus limits its contacts with the media. The media come to the staff; rarely does the staff seek out publicity.

Major Problems Encountered in Investigating Complaints

Getting information directly from nursing home residents is facilitated by the regular visits of the ombudsman to the nursing home. It takes time, however, for the ombudsman to gain the resident's confidence and trust.

Residents frequently fear reprisals from facility personnel for voicing their complaints. Since the ombudsman is an "outside individual" who visits the facility regularly, the resident can express concerns confidently and confidentially, without fear of reprisal.

Generally, the ombudsmen have little difficulty in taking care of issues solicited within the facility. Problems do arise, however, when contact with regulatory or service agencies (i.e., financial difficulties with Medicare or Medicaid) is involved. Prompt settelent is usually hampered by bureaucratic red tape. No ready solution has as yet been found for this problem. Some success has been achieved by establishing informal relationships with key personnel of the home. Personal pressure by the state director of NHOP on key service agency personnel has also had some impact, but this approach is not readily adaptable to most situations.

In cases where the ombudsman's efforts have been exhausted and the only recourse has been to refer the complaint to the State Department of Public Health, problems have been encountered with the state's ineffective investigation, verification, and resolution procedures.

While the Michigan Department of Public Health will investigate concerns, its investigative procedure is of questionable thoroughness. When complaints are verified, its action is usually limited to a hand-slapping letter to the facility, accompanied by a list of recommendations for future implementation. Almost no attempt is made to rectify the situation; thus, whatever investigation occurs does not settle the original complaint to the satisfaction of the complainant.

Public hearings on the department's inability to enforce the state's laws and regulations on nursing homes were conducted in March 1975. The results are still pending.

Roles of the Ombudsman: Case Examples

1. The Lansing unit received a complaint from a local unit accusing rural physicians of charging the Medicaid patient's protected income funds, as well as their families, for medical visits to supplement the amount reimbursed them by Medicaid. This practice began because rural physicians were reimbursed only six dollars per patient visit versus the ten dollars urban physicians were getting.

The state director of NHOP filed a complaint with the State Department of Social Services, requesting an investigation of the procedure. NHOP's position was that if a doctor accepted Medicaid patients, he had to accept what the state paid for the visits; could not deduct medical care costs from the patients' protected income funds; and could not force relatives to pay for medical charges covered by Medicaid. NHOP also questioned the four dollar discrepancy in reimbursement.

NHOP also maintained that once a doctor accepted patients, he had to bill Medicaid for all medical costs. It was discovered, however, that the Michigan Department of Social Services had no such policy. Since a far-reaching policy directive was being formulated, the complaint was reviewed by the director of Social Services, who, in turn, requested an interpretation from the state attorney general.

As a result of NHOP efforts, the director of the Department of Social Services sent a letter to all service providers stating that any physician who accepted Medicaid patients *must* bill Medicaid for all medical costs, and that physicians were prohibited from billing patients, their protected income funds, or their relatives for services covered by Medicaid.

Regarding the four dollar discrepancy in reimbursement rates, NHOP learned that fees are set according to geographic location, population density, and the economic status of the area. Thus, the discrepancy stood.

2. NHOP has been active in several cases in which a profit-making organization sought to purchase a county medical care facility but could not because area citizens protested the sale.

The first involvement in this area occurred when the president of the County Senior Citizens Council on Aging requested the Lansing office's assistance in saving the county medical care facility from profit takeover. Information was obtained on the ownership of the corporation that was trying to buy the facility; such data included present facilities owned and their locations, and the licensing and certification reports on the facilities. A meeting was arranged with the Department of Social Services to gather more information on the sale. NHOP opposed the sale on the basis that the county medical care facility had satisfactory survey reports, while all of the corporation's facilities had received consistently poor reports. The State Department of Social Services called the county department and requested that NHOP be allowed to speak at the scheduled hearing on the matter. The request was granted, and a morning meeting (prior to the afternoon hearing with the corporation and county) was arranged with the county department to present NHOP's data to the director and to the County Board of Commissioners.

Attending the afternoon meeting were the county director of Social Services, four commissioners, three local union members, several members of the County Senior Citizens Council, representatives of the corporation, and the state director of NHOP. The corporation members left the meeting when the county began to assert that it would do all in its power not only to retain the county facility, but also to expand it.

After the decision to retain the facility was made, NHOP proposed a way to facilitate its expansion. NHOP suggested that the commissioners and the members at the meeting should extract the top fifty taxpayers—whether farmers or corporations—from the county tax rolls. Next, each of these individuals was to be given an explanation of the need for expanding the facility and the advantages of local versus corporation control. The commissioners' primary objective was to obtain questions from the individuals, and once this was done, the group would sit down and write logical answers to the questions raised. The questions and answers would then be sent back to the respondents. It was hoped that this method would take care of any taxpayer opposition when it was time to raise the taxes needed to obtain funds for expansion. To date, no opposition has been raised, and the county commissioners are proceeding with their tax increase.

3. A former employee (a nurse's aide) who had resigned from a nursing home had contacted her state representative and had reported that the home had violated the patients' visitation rights and right of privacy. The state representative in turn contacted NHOP about possible courses of action. NHOP appointed the complainant an "instant ombudsman." She was instructed to return to the facility, ask to see specifically named patients, and obtain from these patients their written permission for her to speak with them.

When the "instant ombudsman" attempted to gain entry, she was asked to leave. She refused and was then charged with trespassing. The local police department was called and was asked to arrest her. The request was denied, for the arresting officer was her husband.

The nursing home owner-administrator then obtained a court order to show cause as to why she should be arrested for trespassing and to declare that she should be legally restrained from "harassing" residents (even though residents had requested to see her).

Next, the lawyers representing the owner and the district judge who issued the order were contacted. Both were anxious that the case not come to court, holding that the issue could easily be settled without such drastic recourse. The scheduled hearing was suspended, and in its place a meeting was arranged between the nursing home lawyer, the administrator and concerned staff, the complainant, the state representative, and the state director.

A copy of the Patients' Bill of Rights (December 1974) was given to all participants at the meeting. The sections on visitation and privacy were reiterated to those present. After much discussion between the state director, the lawyers, and the owner of the facility, it was agreed that the ombudsman would have free access to the home to visit whomever she wanted and whenever she wanted—anytime between 10 A.M. and 10 P.M., seven days a week. If the resident's room was not sufficiently private, a separate room would be set aside for discussions and meetings. Henceforth, no nursing home personnel would accompany visitors to rooms, and the patients' rooms would not be monitored by the call systems during private visits. If this procedure was not adhered to, NHOP would seek legal redress in district court.

4. The following case was the first instance in which all county agencies worked together to improve conditions in a nursing home.

A number of complaints were lodged against an extended care facility: lack of professonal services, professional training, planned programs, menu planning, adequate food for residents, outside services for residents, and medical personnel following recommendations from a state institution that had placed releasees in the home; and incompetent administration.

NHOP had been working with the home for six months with only mixed results; thus, the assistance of several agencies in upgrading the quality of care in the facility was requested. These agencies were the Washtenaw County Mental Health Board, Washtenaw County commissioners, Washtenaw County Council on Aging, Washtenaw County Departments of Social Services, Public Health, and Mental Health, Ann Arbor Council on Aging, Ypsilanti Council on Aging, Ypsilanti State Hospital, and Ypsilanti City Council.

As a result of these combined efforts, the problem was corrected in weeks. The administrator was relieved of her responsibilities, the registered nurses were asked to resign, the licensed practical nurses were forced to relinquish their positions, and the nurses' aides resigned. If all counties and cities would work together in this fashion, the quality of care in nursing homes would be improved and projects such as NHOP would fold.

5. Over 500 foreign nurses have been brought into Michigan nursing homes

and hospitals by various agencies over the last few years. All foreign nurses must take English proficiency tests—both oral and written—and must have received a nursing degree from an accredited school of nursing. In one year, 80 percent of the nurses who took the state English proficiency exam failed. Nonetheless, nursing homes and hospitals in Michigan still hired these individuals as RNs and LPNs. Without proper knowledge of English, these nurses could not read or understand doctors' orders, write medical reports, and prepare and administer biologicals and drugs. The nurses themselves were taken advantage of by the nursing home industry, for they were paid lower than normal wages.

Unscrupulous agencies that import foreign nationals into the United States charge them exorbitant fees for transportation to America and for housing once they arrive. In addition, the nurses are exploited by their own government, which requires them to return 20 percent of their wages to the government.

In some cases, U.S. university officials go to foreign countries and train nurses in how to pass the English proficiency test. The immigration authorities, meanwhile, are pressuring the state nursing boards to lower state licensing requirements.

The Michigan Senate and House of Representatives, in conjunction with NHOP, are developing legislation to prevent all universities from conducting courses in how to pass the English proficiency test; to *increase* the requirements for licensing registered nurses; to license and monitor all agencies bringing foreign nationals into the state for the purpose of employment; and to make it a felony to hire and employ foreign nationals who are unable to pass the English proficiency test, both oral and written.

Issues in Long-Term Care Delivery

Ineffective Enforcement System

NHOP believes that the Michigan Department of Public Health must have an alternative method to force nursing homes into compliance with state and federal regulations. Currently, when a nursing home is surveyed, found to be in serious violation of regulations, and an intent-to-deny-licensing order is issued, the facility has the right to appeal the decision. The present appeal process has been known to take months—even years—during which time the violations resulting in the intent-to-deny-licensing order are allowed to continue in the facility (unless they are so serious as to endanger the health and safety of the residents).

When numerous deficiencies are found in the licensing and certification survey, but are not sufficiently severe to warrant such drastic action as an intent-to-deny-licensing order, departmental action generally consists of a letter to the facility which recommends certain actions the facility is to "take under advisement."

A home is rarely closed because it creates severe and undue mental anguish for the residents—and sometimes even death. Even so, allowing abominable conditions to continue while a system of threat-appeal drags on is an inexcusable injustice to the residents.

NHOP has reviewed countless numbers of facility evaluation reports and field reports on nursing homes in Michigan. The repeated appearance of the same "minor" violations in these reports over a five- or six-year period constitutes evidence enough that the enforcement system in Michigan is in sad want of revision.

NHOP has been working with the Michigan legislature on a bill that proposes to establish a system of fines to enforce nursing home regulations and to expedite the correction of deficiencies cited by the health department consultants in licensing and certification surveys. This bill is based on similar laws passed in California and Rhode Island, which give a facility a certain time period in which to correct deficiencies; if they are not corrected, no attempts at correction are made, or if the licensing agency is not notified of an intent to comply with regulations, the facility is fined a set amount of dollars per day per violation until the deficiencies are corrected.

Training of Nurses Aides

One of the most common concerns of health care workers is that patient care is too frequently being given by unprepared individuals. Linked to the idea of upgrading the quality of care is that of improving the quality of the person giving that care.

Representatives of the nursing home industry, government agencies, and professional, academic, and consumer organizations involved in long-term care have initiated a statewide program to improve the performance and job satisfaction of nurses' aides through the development of more effective training programs and better working conditions, staffing patterns, and regulatory procedures.

Under the title of the Michigan Committee on Long-Term Care, various committees, subcommittees, and taskforces have been established to study all aspects of the problem. As previously stated, the Lansing unit of NHOP has been particularly active in the training aspect of the study. The Lansing staff has spent several months compiling data on all available training programs for aides and orderlies. The resulting report will be used as the basis for designing a standard statewide curriculum for training aides.

Statewide coordination is definitely needed to resolve such a widespread problem as that of poorly trained aides. If the participating organizations do not become mired in the usual bureaucracies and academic fantasy-lands, a useful program just might develop.

NHOP is now creating legislation that would require the licensing and certification of nursing aides. The bill will not be introduced until further information is gathered on the feasibility of such a requirement.

Nursing Staff-Patient Ratio Requirements

Closely associated with the aide problem is that of an inadequate ratio of nurses to patients.

Michigan has two different requirement ratios. The ratio of nursing personnel (including aides, orderlies, and ward clerks) to patients is 1:8 for the day shift; 1:12 for the afternoon shift; and 1:15 for the night shift. The ratio of licensed personnel to patients is 1:64 for the day shift; 1:96 for the afternoon shift; and 1:120 for the night shift.

The present requirements set a minimum of 15.75 nursing care hours per patient per week.

Early in 1974, the Michigan Department of Public Health asked NHOP to participate in a departmental study of nursing staff ratios in nursing homes. The purpose of the study was to find a flexible means of regulating staff ratios—"to evaluate nursing personnel to patient ratios presently existing and to evaluate the most effective and efficient method of meeting the nursing care needs of the patient."

Facilities that wished to participate in the study (on a strictly volunteer basis) were to submit to the State Department of Public Health an alternative staffing plan and objectives for consideration. The facility would be allowed to deviate from the present total nursing personnel ratios, but not from the licensed personnel ratios. Sample size was set at six facilities. Progress/failure throughout the study would be monitored by the State Department of Public Health nursing consultants and NHOP.

Unfortunately, the study has been postponed until a later date because the department is in the process of rewriting Michigan's rules and regulations on nursing homes. NHOP is encouraging a rescheduling of the study and plans to be involved in it when it begins.

One of the most frequent complaints received by the ombudsmen is that a patient calls for assistance and no one comes—or assistance comes much later than the time it was first requested. The nursing home's usual response is that there is a lack of personnel at the times they are most needed. Hopefully, if and when the study gets under way, one should be able to ask the residents, at the end of the study, if in fact assistance did come when actually needed.

Patients' Bill of Rights

Federal regulations governing the rights of patients in nursing homes were finally released in 1974. Enforcement of the regulations will be difficult, however. First, there are no concrete incentives to encourage implementation, and second, there are no concrete enforcement procedures.

NHOP has already incorporated a section of the bill of rights regulations into its fines-system legislation, but the question is, what will happen with the enforcement of the regulations in the meantime?

Legal Guardianship

One of NHOP's continuing concerns has been in the area of legal guardianship and the nursing home resident. Too frequently, the ombudsman has found that a resident's guardian is a guardian in name only. Attempts to contact guardians for assistance often lead nowhere, and in instances where contact is made, the person refuses to assist with a problem.

Once a guardian is appointed by the court, there is no real incentive for the appointee to take a personal interest in his ward. The real need of most nursing home residents with regard to guardians is to find individuals who will take a personal interest in their overall well-being. An added difficulty is that one court-appointed guardian (generally an attorney) may have literally hundreds of individuals as his charges.

A bill was introduced by the 1975 state legislature that would have been a step toward correcting the present guardianship situation in Michigan. It proposed to establish in each county the salaried position of public guardian to coordinate and follow up on guardianship activities. Such a system currently exists in a few Michigan counties.

The bill did not make it through the legislature. NHOP plans to revise the bill and to reintroduce it. If it is passed, it could conceivably lead to the licensing and certification of guardians.

Criteria for Levels of Care

Another continuing concern has been to determine what level of care an individual needs—or more specifically, to find out what criteria physicians and the State Department of Public Health consultants use in placing an individual or in evaluating the care being given.

No single set of guidelines, federal or state, strictly defines the levels of care available for consideration. There are general criteria, used on the county or state level, but these tend to differ from each other. This leads to a subjective judgment of the condition of the person and to a random selection of the level of care seemingly most appropriate for that person—depending largely on the mood/experience of the consultant or physician and on what is actually available in the area.

This lack of concrete definitions results in frustration and even trauma for the nursing home resident. He is evaluated as fluctuating between levels and is forced to be moved to and from "distinct units" within a facility—or even worse, out of the facility to one providing the level of care the resident was last determined to need.

This procedure is related to the discrepancy in the definitions of levels of care among third-party beneficiaries. A specific ombudsman case best illustrates this problem:

A doctor prescribed skilled care for a hospital patient to be transferred to a nursing home. The patient was transferred to such a home. State Department of Public Health consultants and city health department consultants classified the patient as requiring skilled care. Medicare, however, contended that the patient belonged in basic care and thus it would not cover the cost of skilled care. It based its decision on the fact that its criteria of skilled care were "different" from those of the Departments of Public Health and Social Services. It also based its decision on the "recommended level of care" of the consulting physician and nursing facility involved—even though they had also recommended skilled care. Medicare would not accept the fact that the individual was receiving skilled care and could not be receiving basic care, as they believed he should be, because there were no basic care beds in the facility. Their position was that if he were a basic care patient, the facility would be unable to provide for his care.

There is no ready solution. A uniform set of criteria, specifically defining all levels of care, would be the ideal answer, if it were feasible. However, this would not in itself resolve the common problem of misclassification that now occurs (particularly where state or federal asisstance is involved), because establishing specific criteria for determining levels of care does nothing when the facilities (beds) that provide those levels are not readily available where and when needed.

County Medical Care Facilities

An excellent illustration of the power of citizen involvement and of the truth of the belief that nonprofit homes provide better care than profit homes can be found in the county medical care facility.

The question of what to do with the county medical care facility is being asked in an increasing number of counties in Michigan. Apparently, there are forty such facilities in the state, the majority of which are located in rural areas. As mentioned earlier, the Lansing office has been involved in several disputes in which a private nursing home corporation has offered to buy a county facility (and save tax dollars). If the results of these disputes are any indication of attitudes in other counties, it appears that county medical care facilities will be around for a while longer.

Numerous practical issues must be considered, of course, but citizen involvement is a major factor in decisions on county facilities. With a county facility, there frequently is a strong feeling of personal involvement and investment, particularly by the elderly. The reason for this feeling may be that since the facilities are nonprofit-making, they must be providing better care. Individuals look to the county facility as the only place they would want to go to if their health deteriorated to the point where they would need institutional care. They consider it "their" facility. That attitude has been nurtured by past experiences and current attitudes toward the profit-making nursing home. If the nursing home industry succeeds in its attempts to improve its image, then the takeover of county facilities by the industry might become a reality—but only in the distant future.

Medicaid Transportation

In addition to their difficulty in paying for needed routine services not covered under Medicaid, nursing home residents in Michigan face another barrier: limited means of paying the transportation costs to and from the services.

Technically, transportation costs are covered under the Medicaid program. In practice, however, many nursing home residents are in the midst of a sad situation. They need a service and that service is available—but only outside the facility in which they reside. Neither the facility nor the County Department of Social Services will claim responsibility for the transportation costs.

Generic Substitution Legislation

In August 1974, a bill permitting pharmacists to provide generic substitutes for prescribed drugs, upon client request, became law in Michigan. The law was passed to give the customer the option of purchasing the exact drug a physician prescribes or its generic equivalent, which frequently costs less than the brand name drug. If the physician does not wish a substitute to be made, he need only write "no substitute" on the prescription.

The "average" noninstitutionalized customer will undoubtedly make use of and benefit from the Generic Substitution Act. Whether the state medical assistance program will thereby save countless tax dollars on the cost of drugs for institutionalized Medicaid recipients is questionable. NHOP's limited contacts with physicians handling nursing home residents has revealed one common philosophy: "The state's paying for it . . . why should they [the residents] care?"

Limited Scope of Medicaid-Covered Services

The problem of the limited scope of services provided by Medicaid (and Medicare) is not unique to Michigan. Federal emphasis on skilled nursing care rather than on preventive and basic services is partially to blame for the limited benefits. An additional problem is that not all services necessary for the health and rehabilitation of the patient can be defined as "medical." Social services are no less important to the physical and emotional well-being of the patient than the so-called skilled nursing services.

Nursing home residents are hard hit by the skills-oriented system. A majority of the residents confined to Michigan's intermediate-care facilities do not need to be there. If Medicaid and Medicare would extend their coverage to include basic home health services, these individuals could remain in their own homes rather than have to be admitted to a nursing home for the lack of other alternatives.

Those in nursing homes not only have difficulty in obtaining access to routine dental, hearing, and eye care, but they also frequently find that, if they somehow do manage to obtain such services, they have to pay for them themselves as neither Medicaid nor Medicare covers them.

There is little NHOP can easily do to remedy the situation, outside of actively supporting moves toward a national health insurance program and continuing to encourage the expansion of home health care benefits under the Medicaid program in Michigan.

Impact on Long-Term Care Delivery

Unannounced Inspection of Homes

A survey conducted in early 1974 revealed that most state agencies and departments do not announce licensing and certification inspections. Of the twelve state agencies and departments surveyed, only two were found to announce inspections. One of these was the Michigan Department of Public Health which performs the licensing and certification inspections. As a result of the survey, NHOP created and introduced a bill providing for unannounced inspections of nursing homes and homes for the aged.

To launch this first legislative endeavor "properly," NHOP arranged for a press conference to introduce the bill in a local pet shop. This site was chosen because pet shop inspections were among those unannounced. With the "residents" of the pet shop and at least forty senior citizens and other passersby in attendance, Representative Alma Stallworth and Senator Robert Davis, the primary sponsors of the bill, introduced the bill to the public. This was in January 1974.

After several hectic months of "educating" legislators on the value and necessity of unannounced inspections, the bill was signed into law on April 4, 1974.

Bonding of Nursing Home Administrators

NHOP's second legislative endeavor also met with success. Senate Bill 391 was introduced early in 1973 to provide for the bonding of nursing home administrators, in an amount 1¼ times the average of the patient's protected income funds maintained by the facility. This bill was passed to halt the abuse of the patient's protected income funds by the nursing home—either in commingling private funds with the operating funds of the facility, or in keeping inadequate accounts of the patient's funds.

It is impossible to estimate the amount of private, protected income funds lost as a result of nursing home administration abuses. NHOP viewed this bill as a means of allowing residents to regain lost funds as well as of guaranteeing quarterly accountings of funds to each resident.

Through NHOP efforts, the bill was resurrected from impending death in committee and revitalized. It was signed into law in late December 1974.

Patients' Bill of Rights

In June 1973, all ombudsman project directors met in Washington and developed a Patients' Bill of Rights, which governs the right of patients in nursing homes. After returning to Michigan, the Lansing unit gave a copy of the rights to the chairman of the Standards and Ethics committee of the Michigan Nursing Home Association; the chairman was developing a bill of rights for adoption by his association. The membership adopted a Patients' Bill of Rights, which bore a striking resemblance to NHOP's as part of the association's operating principles and management policies.

When the Michigan Nursing Home Association merged with the Michigan Health Facilities Association to form the Health Care Association of Michigan, the Patients' Bill of Rights became a part of the Code of Ethics of the largest nursing home association in Michigan. (The Health Care Association has almost 33,000 of the 38,000 nursing home beds in Michigan.)

Status of the Nursing Home Resident

Since early 1973, NHOP has been seeking an official opinion from the state attorney general on the status of the nursing home resident. An answer finally came—indirectly.

In 1975, those residing in Michigan's profit-making nursing care facilities (those facilities paying state taxes) became eligible for a homestead tax exemption. Thirty percent of a resident's monthly fee for care is considered an extension of the homestead. This exemption will be particularly advantageous in those cases where one spouse remains at home while the other is institutionalized.

Three-fourths Reimbursement of Intermediate Care

Preliminary research is being conducted to determine the feasibility and savings to the state of providing three-fourths reimbursement of intermediate care for home health care. The plan works as follows:

An individual is evaluated for the level of medical care needed. If the level is determined to be intermediate and if the proper facilities are available through family or friends, three-fourths of the reimbursement rate for intermediate care will go to the family or friend who renders the service. Followup will be according to foster care concepts.

With a total of 22,800 individuals falling into the intermediate-care level, this plan would not only be a great financial saving to the state, but it would also mean an emotional saving by increasing the life expectancy of those so affected by it.

Summary of NHOP Objectives

1. To resolve the concerns of nursing home residents promptly and efficiently.
2. To establish external linkages.
3. To service local units in whatever problems may arise.

4. To relay all information pertaining to health care issues and actions of the State Departments of Public Health, Mental Health, and Social Services, and the legislature from the state to local units.

5. To relay all new laws and regulations originating at the state level.

6. To develop appropriate in-house policies and procedures.

7. To develop publicity and public relations at the state level.

8. To deal with and relate to state agencies and state officials, state media networks, federal agencies at the district or regional level, and other organizations that function at the state level.

9. To research and analyze data from local units.

10. To serve as an information and referral service on long-term care issues.

11. To initiate investigations on matters of appropriate substance.

12. To lobby at the state level.

13. To make recommendations to state and local agencies on long-term care issues.

14. To make recommendations on federal programs when applicable.

15. To explore alternatives to institutional care relative to state and local resources.

16. To solicit and recruit university students throughout the state to aid in program implementation.

17. To recruit volunteers to spread the program throughout the state, utilizing United Auto Workers retirees and retired local presidents in recruitment and training efforts.

18. To deal with all complaints not resolved by local units or those that are outside the geographical boundaries of the local units.

The Nursing Home Ombudsman Program can only succeed when the general public becomes aware of and involved with the many problems facing the elderly in American society today.

14
THE ADVOCACY ROLE OF NRTA-AARP

Steve Mehlman and Duncan Scott

Once a "silent minority" on the American political scene, the nation's 21 million older citizens have become an increasingly powerful political force at all levels of government. Three basic factors have brought about this change: (1) The proportion of persons sixty-five years of age and older in our population is steadily increasing, (2) older citizens are registering and voting in far greater proportions than younger pesons and are becoming more politically astute and involved than ever before, and (3) national and statewide organizations representing the elderly have begun mounting informational and lobbying campaigns utilizing the services of unpaid volunteers as well as paid professionals.

The rapid growth of these advocacy groups since the 1971 White House Conference on Aging and the greater public attention is focused on the needs and desires of older Americans have resulted in increasing pressure on elected officials and candidates to heed and actively court the so-called elderly vote. Yet, this is not the first time that older persons have organized politically to achieve their goals.

"Old-Age" Politics Then

Francis E. Townsend and the Great Depression
Spawned by the Great Depression, several political movements were formed during the 1930s and 1940s, primarily in California, to obtain pensions and other benefits for older persons. Perhaps the most famous of these movements was launched in 1933 by the California physician, Dr. Francis E. Townsend. The so-called Townsend Plan called for the retirement of all Americans aged sixty or older on pensions of at least $150 per month (later raised to $200), provided the retiree spent all of the pension during the same month he or she received it. The plan was to be financed by a national sales tax.

The Townsend movement attracted a nationwide following during the mid-1930s, with Townsend clubs established in every state. (Movement leaders claimed about 1,200 clubs in California alone.) Mass meetings and demonstrations took place throughout the country. At one point, nearly 14 percent of California voters (the balance of power between the Republican and Democratic parties in that state) supported the Townsend Plan. The movement was dealt a severe blow in August 1935, however, with the passage of the Social Security Act. By 1942, as a result of a combination of political ineptitude, internal bickering, factionalism, and charges of corruption, the Townsend movement ceased to exist as a major political force.[1]

Upton Sinclair

During the same period, Upton Sinclair, a Socialist turned Democrat, won the 1934 Democratic nomination for governor of California with a twelve-point program called EPIC (End Poverty in California). The basis of Sinclair's plan was to place impoverished persons on idle land to grow food or in idle factories that they would operate at government expense. Another provision of the EPIC program called for the granting of a $50 per month pension to all needy Californians over sixty years of age who had resided in the state for at least three years.

Despite sometimes vicious attacks by his opponents during the general election campaign, Sinclair might have won the election had he not underestimated the increasing popularity of the old-age pension issue and made a serious political blunder. Following President Franklin D. Roosevelt's promise during the summer of 1934 that he would recommend passage of a national social insurance law by the next session of Congress, Sinclair declared that state action on pensions should be postponed until Congress acted on the Social Security proposal. He thus forfeited the initiative on the issue to his political opponents and undoubtedly lost large numbers of elderly votes.

The EPIC movement continued to exist in California for a number of years after 1934, primarily because of a core of support and the election of twenty-three EPIC candidates to the state legislature despite Sinclair's defeat. A promoter of the aged welfare movement, EPIC played a positive, though relatively inconspicuous, role in old-age politics throughout the 1930s.[2]

"Ham and Eggs"

In the late 1930s, the "Ham and Eggs" plan, involving the issuance of state scrip to supplement federal currency, won large-scale support throughout California, despite the fact that knowledgeable critics labeled the proposal "economic fantasy." With a battle cry of "Thirty Dollars Every Thursday," supporters obtained nearly 800,000 signatures to place the plan on the November 1938 ballot; almost succeeded in having the plan adopted by California voters in 1938 (it lost 1,143,670 to 1,398,999); and forced a special referendum in November 1939 (in which the plan was defeated by over a million votes).

While the leaders of the Retirement Life Payments Association, which controlled the Ham and Eggs movement, were adept at acquiring a large following for their cause, they were apparently equally adept at running a totally centralized, dictatorial organization through which at least some of them obtained considerable financial remuneration. At the same time, thousands of aged members were constantly solicited for funds, deprived of responsible roles within the organization, and denied the opportunity to develop their own leadership. Once the "unity" of the organization began to crumble in early 1940, the movement was, for all practical purposes, finished. This occurred despite a subsequent abortive attempt to recall the governor of California because of his opposition to the Ham and Eggs plan.[3]

These three movements and similarly unsuccessful efforts throughout the 1930s, 1940s, and 1950s had several things in common: they attempted to obtain continued mass support for a narrow, specific proposal; their leaders were basically overbearing and inflexible; and they attempted to inject themselves directly into the political process by running "slates" of candidates favorable to their cause.

"Old-Age" Politics Now: The Broad-based, Nonpartisan Approach

At the present time, several organizations in the United States which are engaged in politics at the national level "are preoccupied, more or less exclusively, with old-age problems."[4] Four of these are trade associations: the American Association of Homes for the Aging, the American Nursing Home Association, the National Council of Health Care Services, and the National Association of State Units on Aging. A fifth organization, the National Council on Aging, represents 1,400 public and private social welfare agencies, and a sixth, the 2,000-member Gerontological Society, is a strictly professional organization. The recently formed National Caucus for the Black Aged concentrates on the problems of aging among the minorities. Finally, there are three "mass-membership" organizations: the National Retired Teachers Association-American Association of Retired Persons (NRTA-AARP), the National Council of Senior Citizens (NCSC), and the National Association of Retired Federal Employees (NARFE). Another group, the Gray Panthers, concentrates most of its socioeconomic and political pressure on institutions at the local level.

Because of a limited pool from which to draw its membership and, therefore, a limited source of income, NARFE has had to concentrate its basic efforts on bread-and-butter issues affecting its own members rather than on the broader economic and social issues affecting the elderly in general.

NRTA-AARP, with nearly 8 million dues-paying members, and NCSC, with about 200,000 dues-paying and 3 million "affiliated" members, do not limit their legislative priorities. While their predecessors in the 1930s focused on more specific issues, NRTA-AARP and NCSC address themselves to the entire range of "aging" problems and, by proposing a wide range of solutions, are able to attract a much broader base of support. Both of the groups, in contrast to the Townsendites, Ham and Eggers, and EPIC supporters of the past, tend to have more flexible leadership structures that adapt more rapidly to changing conditions. In addition, NRTA-AARP and NCSC remain generally nonpartisan and use sophisticated informational and lobbying techniques, rather than directly challenging the two political parties by running "slates" of candidates, to achieve their legislative goals.

Both groups originated, however, in response to specific issues. NCSC was an outgrowth of the fight for congressional enactment of Medicare in the early 1960s, while NRTA was founded in 1947 to help bring about improvements in state pensions and federal tax benefits for retired teachers.

The Growth of NRTA-AARP

While primarily concerned about the insufficient pensions received by her retired colleagues, Dr. Ethel Percy Andrus, founder of the National Retired Teachers Association, was also interested in improving the image and status of all older citizens. Following her forty-one-year career as a teacher and administrator in California's public schools, she campaigned for more than two decades to bring older citizens out of poverty and isolation and into the mainstream of American life. Prior to her death in 1967 at the age of eighty-three, she summarized: "We have demonstrated that old age is not a defeat but a victory, not a punishment but a privilege. We have held ourselves instinctively responsive to the needs of our people. We have become successful social innovators. We have proved that the leisure of the elderly can be a many-splendored thing."[5]

Dr. Andrus was a strong proponent of free enterprise and individual initiative; hence the NRTA-AARP motto: "To serve, not to be served." She tended to rely on the private enterprise system rather than on government intervention to help provide for the material needs of older persons. When this and other membership services proved immensely popular and brought requests for similar benefits from retirees outside the teaching profession, Dr. Andrus founded the American Association of Retired Persons in 1958, an organization open to any person fifty-five years of age and older. (In 1972, a preretirement division of AARP called Action for Independent Maturity was created for working persons between the ages of fifty and sixty-four.)

The two "sister" organizations, which have separate memberships and organizational structures but use a combined professional staff, have shown remarkable growth, particularly in the last five years. In 1959, the combined dues-paying membership of NRTA-AARP was approximately 150,000; ten years later it reached one million. Since 1969, it was increased to nearly eight million and continues to grow at a rate of more than 100,000 new members per month. Of this total, the NRTA membership of approximately 440,000 represents two of every three retired elementary and secondary school teachers in the country.

With the growth of the two organizations has come a change in legislative philosophy and methodology. While Dr. Andrus was a vigorous witness at congressional hearings and helped establish the structure for the 1961 White House Conference on Aging, her organizations were not generally recognized as being special-interest lobbyists during the period prior to 1967. The thrust of the associations during that time reflected a philosophy of endorsing private enterprise in lieu of massive government intervention.

But since the early 1970s, as rapid growth has fostered a wider range of political viewpoints among the membership, the legislative goals of the associations have been expanded to cover a broad spectrum of public policy issues. With retired blue collar workers, civil service and railroad employees, and lower income Social Security recipients joining AARP, its legislative philosophy has become more attuned to the needs and viewpoints of these retirees. The legislative staff of the two associations has expanded to keep pace with the growth in membership; twelve staff members are currently engaged in lobbying efforts in Congress and the executive branch, while another nine are involved in assisting the organizations' volunteer legislative committees at the state level.

Organizational Structure of NRTA-AARP

Possibly learning from the mistakes of previous organizations of older citizens, NRTA and AARP have developed organizational structures that attempt to provide leaders from the ranks of older citizens themselves at local, state, and national levels. Each association has a fifteen-member board of directors, with each director elected to a six-year term. In addition, national officers are elected to two-year terms and are ineligible for reelection to the same office. Once a person has been elected vice-president of AARP or first vice-president of NRTA, succession to the offices of president-elect and president is automatic, thus guaranteeing that the presidents of both organizations will have at least four years of previous experience in national leadership positions.

Executive committees for each organization meet four times a year to deal with administrative and policy matters, and they are consulted at other times on issues requiring urgent action. For administrative purposes, the associations are divided into nine geographic "areas" that approximate the ten regions of the U.S. Department of Health, Education, and Welfare. Each association has an area vice-president, one or more associate area vice-presidents, and state directors for each state and the District of Columbia. All of these are volunteers chosen by the respective executive committees.

At the local level, program activities are carried out by more than 2,100 AARP chapters and more than 2,200 RTA units throughout the country. Each chapter and unit is mandated by its charter to conduct at least a minimum amount of community service activity each year. Each has a legislative chairman responsible for informing the membership of important legislative developments. (See Advocacy at the State Level on page 173.)

Activity at all levels is coordinated by the NRTA-AARP professional staff, headed by an executive director, located in Washington, D.C. (national headquarters), Long Beach, California (western headquarters), and nine regional offices.

Programs to Enhance the Image and Status of the Elderly

Through their programs at state and local levels, AARP and NRTA seek to involve their members in community affairs in order to enhance the image and status of older citizens in the community-at-large. A number of such programs are carried out locally by AARP chapters and RTA units and include crime prevention, health education, driver education, church relations, and tax assistance programs. Although they are sponsored by NRTA-AARP, they are also open to nonmembers.

In addition, chapters and units are encouraged to sponsor or participate in local community-service projects such as Meals-on-Wheels, telephone reassurance, fund-raising, and hospital and nursing home assistance programs. The fact that the charters for all AARP chapters and RTA units require them to participate in at least a minimum amount of public service activity makes these local groups somewhat different from other senior citizens' clubs, which are basically designed for social and recreational purposes. Officials from NRTA-AARP feel that this community involvement gives older citizens increased visibility and helps to build an image of dedication and responsibility that is useful in playing an advocacy role in their communities.

Intergenerational Relations

Most younger persons are reluctant to admit that they are growing old and will someday encounter the same problems that older citizens face today. It is this reluctance that has led to the unfortunate segregation and stereotyping of millions of older Americans and has made the advocacy efforts of organizations for the aged more difficult.

In an attempt to counter this negativism, NRTA and AARP both sponsor preretirement programs designed for working Americans. AARP's preretirement division, Action for Independent Maturity (AIM), offers retirement planning information and benefits to its 200,000 members as well as complete retirement planning seminars to business and industrial firms, churches, and other institutions. The seminars deal with health, finances, psychological and emotional attitudes, and legal matters. A similar retirement education program is offered by NRTA, which works closely with the National Education Association, state education associations, and other organizations of active teachers.

In an effort to promote greater dialogue between young and old Americans, AARP has developed a Generations Alliance Program through which local chapter members meet informally with high school or college-age young people to discuss issues of mutual interest. The purpose of these sessions is to create greater understanding and friendship among persons of different age groups. It is expected that these sessions will facilitate cooperative community-service efforts that may utilize the skills of both younger and older persons.

Publicity

Modern Maturity, a magazine published for members of AARP, includes articles on a wide range of popular subjects, including travel, health, housing, sports, books, humor, and national affairs. Members of NRTA and AIM receive similar bimonthly magazines, the *NTRA Journal* and *Dynamic Maturity*, respectively. The AARP and NRTA *News Bulletin* provides information on national legislative developments and local and state association activities, as well as other news of interest and practical value to members.

In addition, the associations publish a number of informational booklets and pamphlets on various subjects which are available free to the public. Among these are "Tax Facts for Older Americans," which compares the tax treatment of older persons in each of the fifty states. Another available publication lists the NRTA-AARP Federal Legislative Objectives and State Legislative Guidelines. While all of the free publications are helpful in terms of membership promotion, the two listed above serve more of an advocacy than promotional function.

Aging as a Science and an International Concern

With the exception of the professionally oriented Gerontological Society, NRTA and AARP have been the only other advocacy organizations for the aged to become actively involved in the field of scientific aging research. Between 1968 and 1973, NRTA and AARP members contributed some $2 million to the establishment of the Ethel Percy Andrus Gerontology Center at the University of Southern California. Additional contributions by NRTA-AARP members are placed in an Ethel Percy Andrus Memorial Fund, from which grants are provided to the Andrus Center and to other major universities for age-related research.

Both NRTA and AARP are members of the International Federation on Aging (IFA), organized in 1973 by seventeen organizations representing twelve countries. The IFA was established to advance the interests of older persons throughout the world and to provide an international forum for discussion of all aspects of aging and retirement. *Ageing International*, an informational bulletin published quarterly in Washington, D.C., is distributed to member organizations of IFA.

Actions to Discredit the Myths of Aging

In a 1974 address to the annual convention of the National Council on Aging, public opinion pollster Louis Harris described in grim detail youth's image of older persons, basing his analysis on a massive public opinion survey on attitudes toward aging.

"To put it bluntly," Harris said, "the portrait of mature citizens drawn by those who have not yet reached maturity is that of unalert, physically inert, narrow-minded, ineffective, sexually finished old people rotting away in poor health, suffering the miseries of loneliness, without proper medical care, and without enough money to live on." Yet, Harris said, according to an in-depth study of the attitudes of older persons themselves, the prevalent image of aging in America "is a flat and unmitigated libel and downright lie."[6]

The policy of the associations is to have older citizens themselves testify before state legislative committees, provide tax counseling and consumer assistance, and operate the other national and community-based programs. This type of self-involvement is considered a necessary step in enhancing the status of older people. At a minimum, it leads to greater visibility.

Advocacy in National Affairs

Style Reflects Membership

While older Americans tend to vote in greater numbers than younger citizens, there is little evidence to conclude that older persons are more likely to vote as a bloc than other age groups. Examples of bloc voting by the elderly are usually confined to local issues, such as school bond and property tax questions. According to the Survey Research Center at the University of Michigan, the growth of a major political movement in the United States based on the interests of any particular age group is highly improbable. "The individual citizen of any age reacts to his situation as he sees it, and this may lead him to support conservative policies, liberal policies or, with little sense of conflict, both at the same time."[7]

Other attitudinal and political research has discredited the myth that older voters are overwhelmingly conservative in their political views. Political analyst Richard Scammon has pointed out that, to the contrary, older persons have been "only a point or two more Republican" than has the rest of the population in recent general elections. Scammon also has noted that it is the "flexibility" of the elder voter—"his willingness to be persuaded"—that makes his group such a potent political force.[8]

Finally, despite the mass demonstrations during the campaign for Medicare in the 1960s and the activities of the Gray Panthers in the 1970s, most older persons seem to prefer the "traditional" style of politics to the "politics of confrontation" that has become more prevalent in recent years. An NRTA-AARP legislative representative commented on this philosophy in describing a recent trip to Georgia: "While a group of older persons was outside the Governor's office picketing, our people were inside watching him sign the property tax relief measure for which we had vigorously lobbied in the legislature. I can't really say how effective picketing is, but the fact that the Governor was signing our bill is pretty concrete evidence that our method is effective."

The lobbying approach taken by the two largest advocacy groups, NRTA-AARP and NCSC, generally reflects the views of their membership, although both groups have moved away from espousing merely parochial, age-related issues and toward involvement in broader social concerns. NCSC, with the major bloc of its active membership coming from the ranks of retired union members, tends to rely heavily on mass meetings, political "rating" systems, vociferous public statements, and other tactics reflective of the political activity of the AFL-CIO and other major unions. NRTA and AARP, on the other hand, generally use a more moderate approach, relying on testimony and statements to Congress and administrative agencies. letter-writing campaigns on specific issues, and less strident, more educational public pronouncements. Yet, with the exception of a few key issues (to be discussed subsequently), the general legislative positions of the two groups on specific issues of concern to older persons are similar.

Federal Legislation: Organizational Structure and Procedure

The federal legislative objectives of NRTA-AARP are formulated each January by a twenty-member Legislative Council composed of ten members from each association. These objectives, which are ratified by the boards of directors of both groups, are used as the basis for legislative policy throughout the year. The council is divided into five sections: Health, Taxation, Income, Human Environment (including housing and transportation), and National Policy (including specific legislation for the elderly, such as the Older Americans Act, consumer affairs, age discrimination, and mandatory retirement). Each section listens to outside experts on both sides of specific issues before formulating the associations' position on those issues. The recommendations of each section are then approved, disapproved, or amended by the entire council.

During the course of the year, when policy decisions related to major issues must be determined on short notice, the associations' legislative staff is empowered to convene special taskforces composed of association members who have expertise in fields relevant to the issue under discussion. The taskforces use the same procedure as the Legislative Council in their deliberations, and their recommendations are approved by the boards of directors of the executive committees of both associations.

This process, according to NRTA-AARP Executive Director Bernard E. Nash, can be compared to that used by a representative or senator in dealing with specific legislation. Through their election, they are given a vote of trust and confidence by their constituents. No one expects a representative or senator to poll the entire congressional district or state before voting on a particular issue. Instead, he or she is expected to gather all possible information on the issue, to listen to all sides of the debate, and ultimately, to use his or her best judgment in reaching a final decision. Nash writes:

> In the same manner, our Legislative Council—and the special task forces assembled to deal with urgent issues—explore on a non-partisan basis all aspects of proposed legislation, hear responsible spokesmen debate specific points, and finally formulate policies that in their judgment serve the best interests of our members and all other citizens. [9]

LEGISLATIVE STAFF ACTIVITIES

Daily legislative activity at the federal level is carried out by a twelve-member staff at NRTA-AARP national headquarters in Washington. Each professional staff member is assigned particular legislative subjects and is responsible for monitoring congressional and executive branch activities, preparing testimony and written statements for hearings, and keeping key officials informed of the associations' positions.

In recent years, the legislative staff has prepared detailed position papers on a variety of often complex legislative subjects, including federal tax laws, the economy, and the energy crisis. It has also gained expertise in evaluating and bringing about changes in federal regulations. These regulations, which are drafted by administrative agencies for use in implementing federal laws, can often mean the difference between the success or failure of major programs established by the Congress. Yet, despite their vital importance, these regulations are usually ignored by the general public and by many Washington lobby groups as well.

NRTA-AARP members throughout the country are informed of legislative developments at the federal level through the associations' *News Bulletin* and magazines. In addition, a special legislative newsletter is prepared by the legislative staff and is sent to the volunteer leadership of both associations, the members of all NRTA-AARP joint state legislative committees, and all AARP chapter and RTA unit legislative chairmen.

Political Pressure: Low Key but Effective

What makes the public policy positions of NRTA-AARP so important to elected officials is the simple fact that members of both associations live in every congressional district and in every state. Like other older persons, these individuals vote in large numbers. As a group, they tend to be better informed voters. While this does not guarantee that a representative or senator will always support NRTA-AARP recommendations, it usually means that the associations' views will receive fair hearings.

In addition to testimony before congressional committees, NRTA and AARP use a number of other methods to help bring other favorable action on legislation. Sponsors of legislation reflecting association positions are often mentioned in the publications. Specific issues of major importance are explained in in-depth articles in the *News Bulletin* and magazines. Members are often asked to write to their own representatives and senators or to the members of a key House or Senate committee and to urge passage of legislation. (Rather than asking members to use form letters, which are easily recognized and usually ignored by congressional offices, NRTA and AARP urge their members to write their own letters in their own words, mentioning the fact that they belong to one of the associations.) When possible, the results of committee and floor votes on major legislation are published in the *News Bulletin*. When one or two key legislators are in a position to determine the success or failure of specific legislation, members of the volunteer leadership from the legislator's home district or state are asked to contact him or her directly.

All of this lobbying activity is done on a strictly nonpartisan basis. When compared to the infamous "arm-twisting" techniques brought to light during Watergate-related investigations, such tactics may appear to be too low key to be effective. Quite often, however, when a representative or senator realizes that significant numbers of older persons in his district or state will be supporting a particular position and will be informed of how he or she voted in the issue, more pressure is unnecessary.

Federal Legislative Objectives

In the field of health care, NRTA and AARP strongly support the establishment of a national health care program that will offer comprehensive, quality health care to all Americans, regardless of age or ability to pay. The associations have urged prompt enactment of the Comprehensive Medicare Reform Act, drafted by the NRTA-AARP legislative department over a two-year period and introduced in both the 93d and 94th Congresses by Senator Abraham Ribicoff (D-Conn.) and a number of House members. This legislation is designed to expand health services available to the elderly or handicapped, reduce or eliminate co-payments by low-income beneficiaries, incorporate the state-run Medicaid program into the federal Medicare program, and provide, for the first time, coverage of prescription drugs, eyeglasses, and other health care items under Medicare.

PRENEGOTIATED FEES

A unique feature of the legislation would require that all fees charged by doctors and other practitioners participating in the program be prenegotiated and that all budgets for hospitals and other institutions be predetermined and approved prior to their participation in the program. (The procedure for prenegotiating fees and preapproving hospital budgets would require the involvement of consumers in the decision-making process.) This aspect of the program would be designed to cut health care costs and curb abuses.

REFORM IN HEALTH CARE

Although both NRTA-AARP and NCSC favor a comprehensive national health plan for all citizens, the Medicare reform legislation supported by

NRTA-AARP has led to a major difference of opinion between the two organizations. NCSC, which strongly supports the Health Security Act (Kennedy-Griffiths) national health plan, has urged the Congress to settle for nothing less and has charged that the Comprehensive Medicare Reform Act is a weak, unnecessary measure that would benefit the insurance interests. NRTA and AARP contend that millions of older citizens need adequate health care now and that they "cannot and should not have to wait for improvement of present government programs that are failing to meet their needs." [10] The associations also point out that the treatment of private insurers under the Comprehensive Medicare Reform Act is more stringent than the regulations included in the original Medicare Act, which was strongly supported by NCSC.

Other health care measures recommended by NRTA-AARP include the establishment of a national policy on long-term care; expansion and strict enforcement of regulations covering nursing homes and similar institutions; greater emphasis on home health services as an alternative to institutionalization; expansion of government efforts in the mental health field; creation of minimum federal standards for private health insurance policies; and legislation to permit the use of generic drugs and allow price posting and advertising of prescription prices by pharmacies.

INCOME

Among NRTA-AARP's income-related recommendations are opposition to any reduction or delay in scheduled cost-of-living benefit increases under the Social Security and Supplemental Security Income (SSI) programs; support for use of general tax revenues rather than increases in the Social Security wage base or tax rate to help finance specific benefit increases and increases in the cost of Medicare; improvement in SSI benefit payments and administrative procedures; ultimate elimination of the Social Security earnings test; and a feasibility study by the Bureau of Labor Statistics to determine the need for a separate Consumer Price Index (CPI) for the elderly. (The CPI is used to trigger cost-of-living increases in Social Security and other income-maintenance programs.)

ENERGY

Among key recommendations in the energy field are the establishment of an independent public corporation to explore and develop energy reserves on federal property; creation of an independent federal office responsible for collecting and analyzing data on existing resources, inventories, prices, production costs, and related information on all energy sources; and thorough reform of the existing loophole-ridden tax laws which apply to the petroleum industry.

TAX RELIEF

Economic proposals call for "substantial and permanent" tax relief for low- and moderate-income persons not conditioned on actual tax liability (more than half of all older persons have no federal income tax liability) and reim-position of price controls on the health care industry until Medicare or national health insurance legislation that would deal effectively with the problem of rising health care costs is enacted.

Other major recommendations include improvements and expansion of public transportation systems; annual construction of at least 120,000 new housing units for the elderly; increased funding for nutrition programs; expansion of the Food Stamp Program; establishment of strong federal standards for no-fault automobile insurance; increased funding for the Consumer Product Safety Commission; creation of an independent Consumer Protection Agency; protection of older workers through inclusion of age as a protective category under the Civil Rights Act of 1964; abolition of the statutory age limit of sixty-five from the Age Discrimination in Employment Act of 1967; and prohibition of a mandatory retirement provision in any employment agreement or contract.

RETIREMENT

The issue of mandatory retirement and age discrimination is another in which NRTA-AARP and NCSC seem to have basic differences of opinion. NRTA and AARP claim that mandatory retirement and age discrimination at any age are unconstitutional, and oppose any barrier that prohibits an individual from working as long as he or she is willing and able physically and mentally to perform his or her tasks. Such barriers, according to NRTA-AARP, include mandatory retirement, limitation of the Age Discrimination in Employment Act to persons between the ages of forty-five and sixty-four, and the Social Security earnings (retirement) test. NCSC, perhaps reflecting its strong support by the AFL-CIO, opposes elimination of the retirement test (while favoring a liberalization) and has not taken strong positions on expanding the Age Discrimination Act or outlawing mandatory retirement.

Advocacy at the State Level

A New Forum

Since the beginnings of the New Deal era, political power in America has flowed inexorably toward Washington, D.C., and away from state and local governments. In the early 1970s, however, President Nixon's New Federalism proposals and congressional enactment of revenue-sharing legislation started a movement toward placing more power and responsibility in the hands of state and local officials. This trend has provided advocacy groups with a few forum and with new opportunities to help improve conditions for the nation's older citizens.

NRTA-AARP first recognized the potential of state-level advocacy efforts in early 1970, and in that year established, on an experimental basis, joint state legislative committees, composed of members of both associations, in California, Florida, New York, and Indiana. The program was established on a permanent basis the following year. At the present time, NRTA-AARP joint state legislative committees are operating in forty-nine of the fifty states (all but Kentucky).

In conjunction with the establishment of these committees, NRTA-AARP sponsored two major conferences of state and local leaders in Washington—the National Forum of State Legislators on Older Americans in December 1972, and a similar forum for local officials in December 1974. These meetings, held in cooperation with the U.S. Administration on Aging and other organizations, were credited with making state and local officials more aware of the needs and abilities of older Americans.

Joint state legislative committees in a number of states have already achieved noteworthy results. The Florida committee, for instance, saw the state legislature enact all of its legislative goals in 1974, including an increase from $5,000 to $10,000 in the state's homestead exemption, a mobile home "bill of rights," a new condominium law requiring full disclosure, substantial reform of the probate code, and legislation permitting the advertising of prescription drug prices. The Connecticut committee successfully urged creation of the nation's first Public Hospital Commission to review the rates and efficiency of the state's hospitals, and it proposed successful legislation requiring the payment of interest to consumers on mortgage escrow accounts and rental security deposits. California, Illinois, Massachusetts, Michigan, New Jersey, New York, Ohio, Pennsylvania, and Texas have also enacted significant legislation for the elderly, supported by the NRTA-AARP committees.

At the same time, state-level advocacy has also produced a dramatic increase in the number of state administrative departments for the aging—from twenty-one in 1965 to fifty today. Three of these departments—in Massachusetts, Connecticut, and Illinois—are at cabinet level. The growth of these administrative departments in recent years has, in fact, resulted in the creation of still another advocacy group: the National Association of State Units on Aging.

State Legislation: Organizational Structure and Procedure

The state legislative goals of NRTA-AARP are determined by the joint state legislative committees, which follow guidelines established by the Legislative Council at its annual meeting. (See Advocacy in National Affairs on page 168.) Each state committee is responsible for monitoring the activities of the state legislature, testifying in support of legislation, and informing association members of legislative developments. Through state newsletters, press releases, articles in the associations' publications, and personal contacts with AARP chapter and RTA unit legislative chairmen, the state committees are able to keep members informed and to provide grass roots support for specific legislation.

State Legislative Guidelines

Recognizing that different conditions exist in different states, the NRTA-AARP Legislative Council each year determines a number of general guidelines which each state legislative committee is to follow in formulating its own specific goals.

In the health care field, the guidelines call for expansion and improvement of the Medicaid program, strict licensing and inspection procedures for nursing homes, creation of day care centers and other alternatives to institutionalization, and training and utilization of paramedical personnel. In other areas, state tax recommendations include tax relief for low- and moderate-income older citizens, improvement of property tax administration and assessment and appeal procedures, tax-free transfer of property between spouses, and exemption of food, pharmaceuticals, and utility bills from sales taxation. In addition, income proposals include tighter controls on public and private pension plans to assure full funding and actuarial soundness, interstate and intrastate portability of public pension service credits, establishment of disability benefit programs for persons over age fifty-five, and increased state support of the SSI program for the aged, blind, and disabled.

Other state recommendations include more extensive provision of public transportation, particularly during off-peak hours and in rural and suburban areas; creation of state housing finance and development agencies to encourage public, private, and nonprofit housing programs; mandatory consumer representation on all state regulatory commissions and agencies; indemnification to victims of violent crime and orientation programs prior to court appearances for older persons called as witnesses; and passage of the Uniform Probate Code to help expedite the handling of estates.

Conclusions

The last five years have witnessed a marked change in attitudes toward older citizens. The almost total preoccupation with youth during the decade of the 1960s has given way to increased interest in the elderly by the media and the general public.

Much of this change has been brought about by the efforts of advocacy groups like NRTA-AARP and by the rapid rise of the elderly's political power and influence at all levels of government. Much of it has come from the gradual erosion of myths and long-held stereotypes about older persons. For example, research by Dr. James Birren indicates that older persons not only have the ability to learn as well as younger persons, but also, in many cases, are able to think more efficiently because they tend to concentrate more quickly on what is crucial to a situation and to ignore details that are not pertinent.

But in the final analysis, the change in attitude toward older persons may be coming about because, quite simply, there are more older persons in our society than ever before. Americans are living longer, and expected breakthroughs in medicine during the remaining years of this century may bring further dramatic increases in longevity. At the same time, the birth rate is sharply declining. Together, these factors mean that older persons will make up an increasingly larger proportion of the total population in years to come.

The lifestyle of older citizens is also changing significantly. According to University of Chicago professor Robert J. Havighurst, "twentieth century technology has produced a revolutionary difference in the lives of elderly people in the past 50 years. They have much more free time and much more money at their disposal than their parents had. This gives them more options, and they are now experimenting with those options." [11] The impact of these demographic and social changes on our economy and other aspects of our daily lives will be enormous. It is just now beginning to be understood by our leaders in government and the private sector.

In her classic work, *The Coming of Age*, Simone de Beauvoir indicts many societies, including our own, for what she sees as cruel indifference toward older persons. She notes that Western societies care about the individual only insofar as he or she is "profitable." She urges a drastic revision of our attitudes toward the old. [12]

Prior to the 1971 White House Conference on Aging, the editors of *Modern Maturity* magazine offered a "Declaration of Aging Rights" as a rallying point for the delegates to the conference:

> We declare that all people inalienably possess these rights without regard to age:
> 1. The right to live with sufficient means for decency and self-respect.
> 2. The right to move about freely, reasonably and conveniently.
> 3. The right to pursue a career or interest without penalty founded on age.
> 4. The right to be heard on all matters of general public interest.
> 5. The right to maintain health and well-being through preventive care and education.
> 6. The right to receive assistance in times of illness or need or other emergency.
> 7. The right to peace and privacy as well as participation.
> 8. The right to protection and safety amid the hazards of daily life.
> 9. The right to act together to seek redress of grievances.
> 10. The right to live life fully and with honor—honor not for age but for humanity. [13]

Three years later, in his speech to the National Council on Aging convention, pollster Louis Harris cited similar sentiments expressed by the nation's older citizens: "Give us less pity and give us more opportunity; give us respect not simply for having lived so long, but respect born of what we are and still can be, much more than we have been; do not count us out; do not put us on the ash heap, wringing your hands all the way to the graveyard about our aging miseries."[14]

Notes

1. Jackson K. Putnam, *Old-Age Politics in California* (Stanford, Calif.: Stanford University Press, 1970), pp. 49-71.

2. Ibid., pp. 34-48.

3. Ibid., pp. 89-114.

4. Henry J. Pratt, "Old Age Associations in National Politics," *The Annals* (September 1974): 106-119.

5. National Retired Teachers Association and American Association of Retired Persons, *Power of Years: The Wisdom of Ethel Percy Andrus* (1968), p. 15.

6. Louis Harris, address given at the National Council on Aging 24th Annual Convention, Detroit, Mich., October 2, 1974.

7. Angus Campbell, "Politics Through the Life Cycle," *The Gerontologist* (Summer 1971): 117.

8. Richard Scammon, address given at the National Forum on Aging for Local Officials, Washington, D.C., December 12, 1974.

9. Bernard E. Nash, "AARP Task Forces Respond Rapidly to Vital Aging Issues," AARP *News Bulletin* (February 1975): 6.

10. Bernard E. Nash, "Health Care Bill Proposed by AARP Is an Urgent Need," AARP *News Bulletin* (April 1974): 6.

11. Robert J. Havighurst, "The Future Aged: The Use of Time and Money," *The Gerontologist* (February 1975): 15.

12. Simone de Beauvoir, *The Coming of Age* (New York: G. P. Putnam's Sons, 1972).

13. "Declaration of Aging Rights," *Modern Maturity* (October-November 1971): 22.

14. Harris, op. cit.

CONTRIBUTORS

Willis Atwell first came to Washington to become executive assistant to the director of the American Association of Retired Persons and later served as associate director of that same organization. He is presently director of field liaison staff for the Administration on Aging.

Lorin A. Baumhover is director of the Center for the Study of Aging at the University of Alabama and is a member of the faculty of the School of Social Work where he teaches research. Dr. Baumhover was educated at St. John's University of Minnesota, at the University of Nebraska, and at Colorado State University where he holds a Ph.D in sociology. He has completed a number of demographic studies of elderly populations in both the southern Appalachians and in the South and is a frequent participant in national conferences.

William V. Bradley has been director of the Ombudsman Program in South Carolina since its inception in 1972. Mr. Bradley's experience also includes administration of long-term care facilities. He is presently active on a number of state committees directed toward improving legislation and policy implementation for the state's elderly population. He was educated at Furman University, Greenville, South Carolina, and at Tulane.

Lillian Colby is executive director of FOCUS on Senior Citizens, a multipurpose planning and service organization, in Tuscaloosa, Alabama. She holds an M.S. in social psychology from Purdue University and has also received specialized education in aging at the University of Alabama.

Nancy Derrington is on the faculty of Bessemer State Technical College where she coordinates Title IV-B training funds in association with the Alabama Commission on Aging. She was formerly nutrition project director (Title VII) for the West Alabama Planning and Development Council, aging programs. Ms. Derrington was educated at the University of Alabama.

Gerald L. Euster is associate professor at the University of South Carolina, College of Social Work. Dr. Euster has worked with the elderly as a staff member of the Menninger Clinic, Topeka, Kansas. He was director of group services at Magee Rehabilitation Center in Philadelphia and a social work training specialist at Philadelphia State Hospital. Dr. Euster has published numerous articles in professional journals and recently contributed to the book *Contemporary Social Work*. In recent years, he has been a consultant to the American Health Care Association and HEW in their revision of an activities coordinator's guide for personnel working in long-term care facilities for the elderly.

Jerry E. Griffin is a native of the rural South. He has organized volunteer services in mental health and mental retardation programs in the South and in New England. He was an executive director of the Greater Boston Association for Retarded Children and later organized and directed a community action agency (funded by OEO) in Alabama. He holds the M.S.W. degree from Boston College and a Ph.D. in administration from the University of Alabama. He is currently associate professor at the University of Alabama School of Social Work.

N. Philip Grote is chief research associate at the Center for the Study of Aging and is on the faculty of the School of Social Work at the University of Alabama. He has studied at Wofford College and at the University of Alabama where he is completing a doctoral program emphasizing volunteerism and evaluative research. Active in the Association of Voluntary Action Scholars, he has presented papers on the education of volunteer professionals and has designed academic and applied curricula in the areas of volunteerism and social services. Mr. Grote has also conducted extensive field research studies on the elderly in Alabama.

Catherine B. Healy is coordinator of the Older Americans Volunteer Programs for ACTION in Region IV with offices in Atlanta, Georgia. Ms. Healey was educated at the University of Georgia and at Tulane where she earned an M.S.W. Her professional experience includes extensive and varied work in volunteerism. Her work was officially recognized by a presidential letter of congratulations regarding volunteer programs in Georgia.

Amelia B. Heath has been director of the Retired Senior Volunteer Program in Tuscaloosa, Alabama, since 1973. Educated in the areas of social services and gerontology at the University of Alabama, Ms. Heath is active in community social services with special interests in volunteerism and volunteer education. She is president of the RSVP Directors Association of Alabama and has served as a member of the In-service Education Committee for Action.

Carol Hill is director of aging programs for the West Alabama Planning and Development Council. Ms. Hill has worked as a psychiatric social worker in a geriatric ward, as a staff member of an OEO community program for the elderly, and as a human resource planner for aging programs. She was educated at Stillman College, the University of Alabama, and Atlanta University.

Solomon G. Jacobson was educated at the City University of New York and at the University of Michigan where he is presently completing a dissertation on resource policy. He is lecturer and project director, Department of Health Planning and Administration, University of Michigan.

James R. Jones is head of the Community Services Division of the United Planning Organization, Washington, D.C. Formerly director of the South Alabama Area Agency on Aging, Mr. Jones holds an M.B.A. from the University of Alabama and has done extensive research in the analysis and use of the area agency proposal as a management tool. Mr. Jones has also served as consultant to the Administration on Aging in the area of service delivery to the rural elderly and has done in-service training for ACTION.

Joan Dechow Jones is an associate professor and director of the Gerontology Program at Antioch College, Columbia, Maryland. Dr. Jones holds a Master's degree in English and an M.S.W. with a Specialist in Gerontology Certificate from the Institute of Gerontology, Wayne State University/The University of Michigan, as well as a Ph.D. (Administration) from the University of Alabama. Dr. Jones is a frequent conference participant and has done longitudinal research on the Title VII Nutritional Program in Alabama; this research provided the basis for her dissertation. Dr. Jones is a former state trainer and educational consultant to the Alabama Commission on Aging.

Steve Mehlman is manager of the editorial services department of the National Retired Teachers Association and American Association of Retired Persons. Prior to coming to the Association in 1971, he was press secretary for U.S. Representative Robert N. Giaimo of Connecticut and a reporter for the *Courier-News* in Plainfield, New Jersey. He is a graduate of the American University in Washington, D.C.

Phillip L. Nathanson has served as state planner for the elderly for the state of Colorado since 1972. His experience includes extensive work in social services delivery, community organization, and training for a wide range of age groups from youth to older adults. Presently, his work involves programmatic planning for almost all aspects of services for the Colorado Division of

Services for the Aging. Mr. Nathanson's undergraduate work in psychology was done at the University of California at Berkeley, and his M.S.W. was earned at the University of Washington at Seattle.

Duncan Scott is a retired foreign service officer now employed as a senior editorial specialist at NRTA-AARP. During twenty-one years with the U.S. Information Agency, he served in Washington, Karachi, Tokyo, London, and Calcutta. He started his career as a newspaperman, taught English and journalism at three colleges, and was an information specialist for the U.S. Department of Agriculture. During World War II he was an officer in the U.S. Naval Reserve.

Deborah Tyra was educated at the University of Alabama and is the nutrition project director with the West Alabama Planning and Development Council, aging programs, Tuscaloosa, Alabama.

Charles H. Waller, Jr., received his M.S.W. and Specialist in Gerontology Certificate and did doctoral work in gerontology at the Institute of Gerontology, the University of Michigan. Active in Citizens for Better Care, an independent advocacy group for persons in long-term care facilities, he became Michigan's Nursing home ombudsman when that organization received a grant to initiate the ombudsman project. Mr. Waller is presently working for the Michigan Republican party in the area of legislation and policy-making for dependent age groups.

INDEX

About the Editors

Lorin A. Baumhover is Director of the Center for the Study of Aging at the University of Alabama and a member of the faculty of the School of Social Work. He has completed a number of demographic studies of elderly populations.

Joan Dechow Jones is an associate professor and Director of the Gerontology Program at Antioch College. A frequent conference participant, she is a former state trainer and educational consultant to the Alabama Commission on Aging.